THE GREAT REVIVAL IN THE WEST
1797–1805

THE GREAT REVIVAL IN THE WEST

1797-1805

By
CATHARINE C. CLEVELAND

WIPF & STOCK · Eugene, Oregon

Wipf and Stock Publishers
199 W 8th Ave, Suite 3
Eugene, OR 97401

The Great Revival in the West
1797-1805
By Cleveland, Catherine C.
ISBN 13: 978-1-60608-591-2
Publication date 4/9/2009
Previously published by Peter Smith, 1916

PREFACE

The Great Revival in the West at the end of the eighteenth and during the early years of the nineteenth century is one of a series of religious movements which shook the religious life of the Colonies and the United States to the foundations. The first of this series was the so-called Great Awakening of 1740, which began about 1735 under the preaching of Jonathan Edwards. The end of that century witnessed the beginning of another great revival, the western phase of which, often spoken of as the Kentucky Revival, is treated in the following pages. Similar movements stirred the country about 1830 and again about 1850.

It is impossible to understand the religious life of the United States without bearing in mind the revival spirit which has from time to time swept over the country. The word revival, however, must not be confined to these greater movements. It recurs frequently in the history of various denominations in the years intervening.

It is the purpose of the present volume to show the importance of the great western revival which occurred between the years 1797 and 1805. In order that the movement may be more clearly understood, the general social and economic conditions of life in the West at the end of the eighteenth century have been considered in detail.

The revival was characterized by marked emotional features which resulted in extraordinary bodily exercises. These exercises, as the treatise endeavors to show, can be accounted for on physiological and psychological grounds. Since it was in this revival that camp-meetings originated, the character of the early meetings merits attention.

The influence of the revival upon the moral tone of the regions affected, upon the denominational life of the West, and upon the general religious life of the country, is an important consideration to the student of United States history, and has been dwelt upon at length.

This work was entered upon some years ago under the general guidance of Professor J. F. Jameson, then professor of history at the University of Chicago. To Professor Jameson, I am greatly indebted for many valuable suggestions in the course of my investigations. To Professor William E. Dodd, I am also under great obligations for valuable suggestions and for his introduction to this volume. The present volume has been accepted as a doctoral dissertation by the Department of History of the University of Chicago.

The materials drawn upon for the study are given in detail in the bibliography.

CATHARINE C. CLEVELAND

CONTENTS

	PAGE
INTRODUCTION	xi
I. THE RELIGIOUS CONDITION OF THE WEST PRIOR TO 1800	1
II. THE REVIVAL LEADERS: THEIR TEACHINGS AND METHODS	34
III. THE SPREAD OF THE REVIVAL AND ITS CULMINATION	62
IV. PHENOMENA OF THE REVIVAL	87
V. THE RESULTS OF THE REVIVAL	128

APPENDIXES

I. James McGready—Testimony of Ninian Edwards before a Committee Appointed by the Transylvania Presbytery, February 12, 1807 . . . 163

II. The Revival of 1800—One of the Favorite Hymns, "Mercy of God" . . . 164

III. Copy of a Letter from Ebenezer Cummins, July 7, 1802 . . . 165

IV. Rev. John Lyle's Account of Sacramental Meetings at Point Pleasant and Lexington in June, 1801 . . . 174

V. Rev. John Lyle's Account of the Great Cain Ridge Camp Meeting, August, 1801 . . . 183

VI. The Great Revival in North Carolina—among the Baptists of the Kehukee Association . . . 190

VII. "An Account of the Revival of Religio[n Which] Began in the Estern Part of the State of Kentuckeye in May 1801" . . . 196

VIII. Letter from William McKendree . . . 202

BIBLIOGRAPHY . . . 206

LIST OF MAPS

FACING PAGE

I. THE WEST: DISTRIBUTION OF POPULATION IN 1800 1

II. PRESBYTERIANS IN THE WEST: APPROXIMATE LOCATION OF PRESBYTERIES IN 1800. . . . 18

III. BAPTISTS IN THE WEST: APPROXIMATE LOCATION OF ASSOCIATIONS IN 1800 20

IV. METHODISTS IN THE WEST: APPROXIMATE LOCATION OF CIRCUITS IN 1800 22

INTRODUCTION

In this story of the Great Revival in the West Miss Cleveland has shown clearly the religious "destitution" of the frontier, the craving of men for excitement, and the effect of powerful emotional appeals upon the minds of simple folk far removed from the main currents of contemporary civilization. While the Great Revival was only one of the many "awakenings" of the people in the early days of the republic, it was, perhaps, the most important of its class and a thorough study of it may suffice for the series of revivals which "raged" in the Middle States, on the southern and western frontier from late colonial times to the War of 1812.

Whether students agree as to the sufficiency of one such study or not, the author certainly presents in the following pages, the best, and I believe, the only scientific account of this important movement. She has studied the subject on the ground, and has read the contemporary newspapers, the journals of preachers, and the minutes of churches, in short all the available records of the revival. And the result is a distinct and positive contribution to our knowledge of the social and moral conditions of primitive life in America. In the chapter on the revival leaders we have brief, concise portrayals of influential men, their manners, ideals, and methods, which add greatly to the value of the study. Nor are the accounts in chapters iii and iv of the "outbreaks" in meetings, the great throngs of people gathered in camps which covered acres of ground, less informing; while for the student of the West and of the frontier during the early nineteenth century the full and painstaking bibliography will prove most grateful.

Having found so much of interest and importance to me in these chapters, I heartily commend the work to all who would like to learn how our predecessors in the United States lived, how they tried to solve moral and religious problems, how they behaved when under the pressure of great emotional appeals. It is a truthful, conscientious, and accurate narrative presented in quiet and dignified form.

WILLIAM E. DODD

UNIVERSITY OF CHICAGO

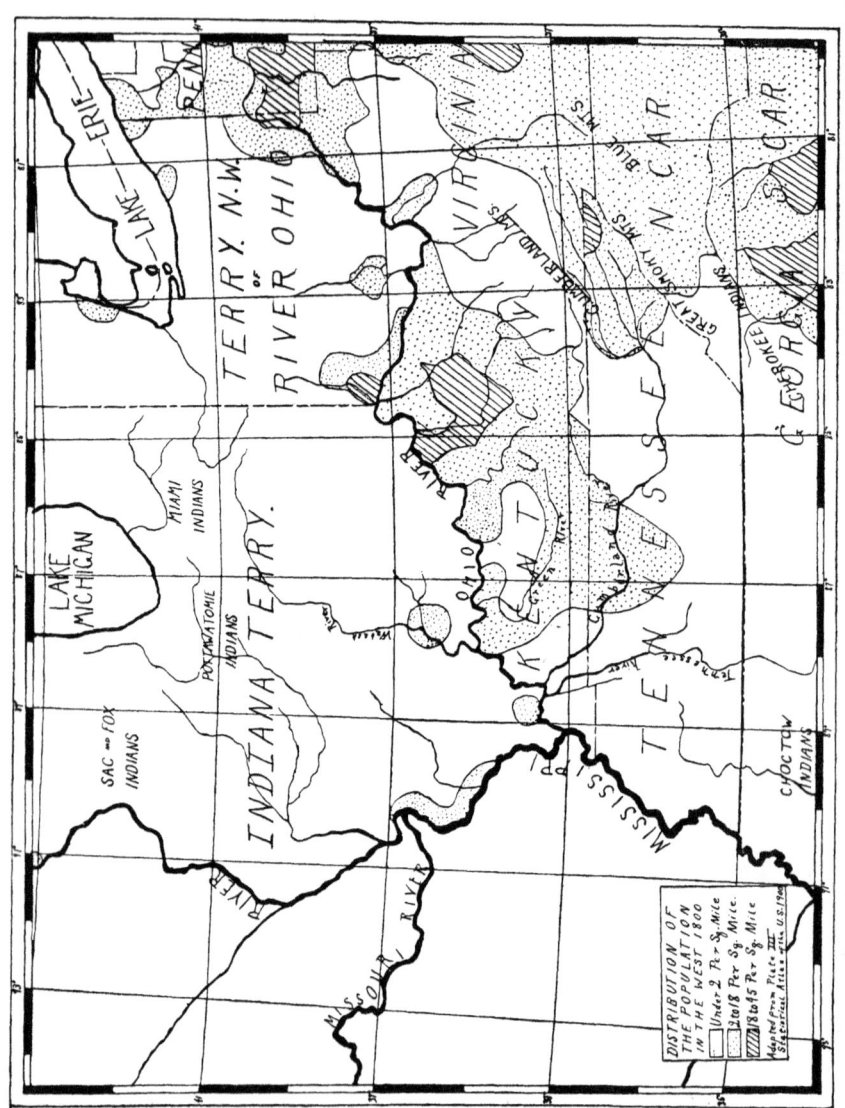

CHAPTER I

THE RELIGIOUS CONDITION OF THE WEST PRIOR TO 1800

By the year 1800, there were to be found in the Alleghany and Ohio valley regions nearly a million inhabitants representing all classes of society and a great variety of nationalities. Nearly every nation in Europe had furnished its quota, each bringing its own peculiarities, yet each actuated by the common desire to better temporal and spiritual conditions in the New World. The streams of Scotch-Irish immigrants which poured in from the north and south met on the frontiers. The rugged mountain country with its fertile valleys suited their agricultural tastes, and here they established homes for themselves and their children. The country west of the Alleghanies, but just beginning to be known a quarter of a century before, had lured many from the states east of the mountains and from the Old World by tales of remarkable fertility of soil and that mysterious and fatal enchantment which always surrounds the unknown.

According to the Census Report for the year 1800 the population of western Pennsylvania, including the region west of the main branch of the Susquehanna River, numbered 274,568; that part of Virginia west of the Blue Ridge, 203,518; North Carolina, west of the Yadkin River, 67,935; Kentucky, 220,955; Tennessee, 105,602; the Northwest and Indiana territory, 51,006 persons of all descriptions.[1] Kentucky and Tennessee had already entered the Union, and Ohio was soon to become a state.

In western Pennsylvania the density of population was greatest about Pittsburgh and the southwestern part of the state bordering on the Virginia and Ohio territory. The settlers in this region had emigrated from Scotland, Northern Ireland, Germany,[2] Switzerland, and from the eastern and southern states of the Union. This country was one of the main highways of travel to the West. Three routes met at Pittsburgh,[3]

[1] United States Census Report for 1800.

[2] Michaux noted in 1805 the air of evident prosperity characteristic of the German settlements. They lived much better than the American descendants of the English, Scotch, and Irish and did not have that unsteady disposition which frequently from the most trifling causes induced them to emigrate (*Travels to the Westward of the Alleghany Mountains*, 63, 64).

[3] "Three routes met at Pittsburgh: one from Philadelphia, by the West Branch of the Susquehanna, a forty-mile portage over the divide and Toby Creek to the Allegheny at Kittanning; a second further south, also from Philadelphia, by the Juniata tributary of the Susquehanna, or by a more direct trace known as Forbes's Road from Carlisle through Shippensburg, Fort Lyttleton, and Fort Bedford to the upper Juniata, thence by an easy mountain pass to the Loyalhanna River by Fort Ligonier

Religious Conditions Prior to 1800

and thence thousands of emigrants floated down the Ohio to form new settlements along its shores or on the banks of the tributary streams.

North of the Ohio, along the Muskingum, the Scioto, and especially the Great and Little Miami rivers flourishing settlements had grown up. New England, Pennsylvania, Virginia, New Jersey, Kentucky, and Tennessee furnished the settlers for this new country.

Across the river in Kentucky, by far the greater number of the inhabitants had come from Virginia. According to Marshall, "one-half of the white people at least and probably three-fourths of the slaves were from Virginia: the residue from the other states, Pennsylvania, Maryland, and North Carolina, furnishing the greater part and in something like a ratio of their own population."[1] Until 1784, immigration to this region had been mainly from the upper country of Virginia, Maryland, Pennsylvania, and the Carolinas. At the close of the Revolution, many officers who had served in the army settled there with their families. Other

and on down the Allegheny, or across the low dividing ridge to the forks of the Ohio, and a third up the Potomac to Fort Cumberland, and thence by Braddock's road over the divide to the Youghiogheny, or to Redstone Old Fort on the Monongahela. This was the natural line of connection with Alexandria and Baltimore." (Ellen C. Semple, *American History and Its Geographic Conditions*, 65).

[1] Marshall, *History of Kentucky*, I, 441, 442.

settlers also came from England, Philadelphia, New Jersey, New York, and the New England states.[1]

In Tennessee, as in the other newly settled regions, the state of society was much diversified. Here were to be found people principally from the Carolinas, from Virginia, and from Georgia, with a considerable number from New England and Europe.[2]

The upper country of Virginia and the Carolinas naturally drew from the coast regions and the foreign immigration directly, and in addition there was a marked drifting of the population from other states.

The pioneer, attracted by the facilities for hunting, had gradually pushed to the westward as his more civilized neighbors followed in his trail, and during the period under survey life in the Allegheny and Ohio valley regions presented certain general characteristics. To the European traveler accustomed to the refinements and luxuries of a settled region and the deference paid to birth in the Old World, there was a crudeness about western life with its rude home furnishings, its lack of social distinctions, its frankness and independence, that often called for criticism.

[1] Imlay, *Topographical Description of the Western Territory of North America*, 137.

[2] Melish, *Travels in the United States of America, 1806, 1807, 1809–1811*, II, 194.

The towns of the day, conveniently located on or near the water-courses, were the centers of life for the surrounding district. A few stores, the jail and court-house combined, perhaps an academy and meeting-house made up the public buildings of the town. Frame houses, which in many instances had replaced the log cabin, gave a general air of prosperity and comfort. Here the country people gathered for trade and gossip, here justice was meted out, and the political situation thrashed over. Court days drew the people in greatest numbers and were marked by much disorderly conduct among the lawless element that congregated at such times and indulged in all sorts of rough amusements, gambling, and heavy drinking. Here, in the tavern and the meeting-house, were represented two opposing elements found in every locality. The largest of the towns boasted comparatively few families; even Pittsburgh had only 1,565 inhabitants, Lexington, 1,797, of whom 439 were slaves, Frankfort, 628, including 260 slaves, Nashville 355, of which number 141 were slaves.[1] The major part of the population was found scattered through the country.

Though great changes had taken place since the pioneer with his gun first penetrated the wilderness, the country was still but sparsely settled, and it was only here and there that the rude log

[1] United States Census Report for 1800.

cabin had given way to the frame house, though it is to be noted that the logs of the pioneer cabin were now more carefully hewn and more neatly plastered than was the case at first. The life of the people who built these cabins is interesting. The bare necessities alone were provided for in many cases. Most of the immigrants desired to better their fortunes and had little to bring with them across the mountains. Then, too, the long and perilous journey forbade the transportation of unnecessary baggage. Once in the wilderness the first thought was of food and shelter. A site was selected for the cabin, trees were felled, and the structure erected as soon as might be. A rude home it was, this log cabin in the wilderness! The furniture was of the simplest kind. A slab of wood set upon hewn sticks did duty as a table, and stools of similar manufacture answered for chairs. Slabs laid across forked sticks inserted in the wall and floor served as bedsteads, though frequently the floor itself, of puncheons, or the uncovered earth, answered the purpose as well. Wooden vessels were used for table service; knives and forks were very scarce, one or two doing duty for the whole family. Game was abundant, and the table was kept bountifully supplied. The ground was broken as soon as possible for the garden, that the winter supply of corn and other vegetables might be assured. Necessity being the mother of invention, the skins of the buffalo and deer served the purpose of dress and coverlets in many instances. Homespun cloth was manufactured by the women and then fashioned by the same hands into various articles of dress.

By the year 1800, some refinements had crept into the western country. Intercourse with the eastern cities was more frequent. Commercial activity had opened a number of stores in the new region, and manufactured articles such as had been known in the older communities were seen in some of the homes. In the towns, stone was sometimes used in the construction of public buildings. Since Wayne's victory, the Indian was no longer a constant dread, and life on the whole was easier. Settlements gradually spread farther away from the river and its tributaries. A marked contrast existed between life in the town and country. Yet for the majority there were still the round of hardship and privation, the loneliness and solemnity characteristic of all sparsely settled regions. Andrew Ellicott wrote on September 29, 1796, of the Ohio settlements:

The buildings on the river banks except in the towns are generally of the poorest kind, and the inhabitants, who are commonly sellers of liquor, as dirty as their cabins, which are equally open to their children, poultry, and pigs. This is generally the case in new settlements, the land being fresh produces with little labour the immediate necessities of life; from this circumstance the habit of industry is diminished and with it the habit of cleanliness.[1]

This same writer thus characterizes the people:

That some turbulent persons are to be met with on our frontiers every person possessed of understanding and reflection must be sensible will be the case as long as we have a frontier and men are able to fly from justice and their creditors; but there are few settlements so unfortunate as to merit a generally bad character from this class of inhabitants.

The people who reside on the Ohio and its waters are brave, enterprising, and warlike (true of all our new settlements). This bravery too frequently when not checked by education and a correct mode of thinking degenerates into ferocity.[2]

Another traveler, in 1803, contrasts the industrious habits of the people living on the west side of the Ohio River with the general shiftlessness of the Virginia side.

Here, in Ohio they are intelligent, industrious, and thriving; *there* on the back skirts of Virginia, ignorant, lazy, and poor. *Here* the buildings are neat though small and furnished in many instances with brick chimneys and glass windows; *there* the habitations are miserable cabins. *Here* the grounds are laid out in a regular manner, and inclosed by strong posts and rails; *there* the fields are surrounded by a rough zig-zag log-fence.[3]

The settlers were grouped by the writers of the period in three classes, according to their social

[1] Ellicott, *Journal, 1796–1800*, 7, 8.   [2] *Ibid.*, 25.

[3] M. Harris, *Journal of a Tour into the Territory North-west of the Alleghany Mountains*, 58.

characteristics and property. The first was that of the pioneer who desired to live apart from men and moved on when "increased immigration disturbed his solitude." Of these, Imlay wrote: "Indeed there is a number of people who have so long been in the custom of removing, farther and farther back as the country becomes settled, for the sake of hunting, and what they call range for their cattle . . . . that they seem unqualified for any other life."[1] Francis Baily speaks of them as "a race of people rough in their manners, impatient of restraint, and of an independent spirit, who are taught to look on all men as their equals, and no farther worthy of respect than their conduct deserves."[2] The second class[3] was a degree above the pioneer, having a little more property and knowing more of the refinements of life. The third class comprised the men and women designated by their contemporaries as "genteel." Accustomed to advantages unknown to the poorer, uncultured immigrant, this class did much to raise the standard of life in the wilderness, and gradually wrought a change in society.[4]

[1] Imlay, *Topographical Description of the Western Territory of North America*, 149.

[2] Baily, *Journal of a Tour in Unsettled Parts of North America*, 217.

[3] *Ibid.*, 218.

[4] For a description of this class in Kentucky, see Baily, *op. cit.*, 237; Imlay, *op. cit.*, 137.

Though the majority of western settlers found the struggle for existence all-engrossing, they recognized the importance of education and early made provision for schools in many localities on both sides of the Ohio River. Academies were established and, in Kentucky especially, were encouraged by grants of land from the legislature. The log schoolhouse by the roadside was a familiar sight in all communities. Here the children of the neighborhood during a few months of the year received such instruction as the chance teacher who offered himself could afford. Lessons were studied aloud; textbooks were scarce, and the mastery of the spelling-book, the primer, the first principles of arithmetic and elementary geography made up the average course of study. The Bible was in great requisition as a textbook, and the catechism was frequently taught.

The following description of a school in Kentucky is interesting:

> In a year or two after our removal, a small school-house was erected by the joint labor of several neighbors. . . . . It was entirely in the woods. . . . . In the winter light was admitted through oiled paper by long openings between the logs. It was one story high, and about sixteen by twenty feet in dimensions, with a great wooden chimney, a broad puncheon floor, and a door of the same material with its latch and string.

In this school the reader was the New Testament, in which the pupils read verse about.[1] The open-

[1] Drake, *Pioneer Life in Kentucky*, 143, 144, 147.

ing of academies, of schools for young ladies, and the readiness of tutors (anxious for employment) to impart knowledge were announced through newspaper advertisements. As early as 1788, spelling-books and readers were offered for sale by western merchants. Many private schools were opened in the homes of ministers who were glad to eke out a livelihood by teaching during the week. In Ohio, as would be expected of New England immigrants, provision was made for the education of the young as soon as a settlement was projected.

The loneliness of life in remote country districts stimulated the desire for human companionship, and fun and frolic at times enlivened the daily round of labor. Spinning-bees, corn-huskings, singing-schools, and similar gatherings ministered to the craving for social life. Weddings were great occasions for hilarity, and dancing was much indulged in by the young people. The older people conversed about the life they had known east of the mountains and compared notes with each other. Imlay gives a picture of social life in Kentucky which, though not applicable to the society generally, is interesting as illustrating the life of the well-to-do in that region.

Flowers and their genera form one of the studies of our ladies; and the embellishment of their houses with those which are known to be salutary constitutes a part of their employment.—Domestic cares and music fill up the remainder of the day, and social visits without ceremony and form leave them without ennui or disgust. The autumn and winter produces not less pleasure. Evening visits mostly end with dancing by the young people while the more aged indulge their hilarity or disseminate information in the disquisition of politics or some useful art or science.[1]

There were, however, those among the serious-minded settlers who looked upon some of the amusements as savoring of frivolity, as incompatible with real earnestness of purpose and contrary to the chief interest of life: the welfare of the soul. Many of the immigrants to the western country had been members in good and regular standing in eastern churches, and while some in the new surroundings forgot all save temporal welfare, others were anxious to continue the enjoyment of privileges to which they had been accustomed and to rear their children in the faith that had meant so much to them. Where the church had emigrated as a body, pastor and

[1] Imlay, *op. cit.*, 139, 140; Bridel, *Description of Kentucky*, 110; "Dans le Kentucky . . . on rencontre beaucoup de personnes qui ont de l'éducation, des connoissances littéraires, des manières agréables et une honnête fortune. . . . En divers endroits, on trouve des assemblées réglées, des cercles, et les autres amusemens des gens comme il faut. Courses à cheval, ou en cabriolet, visites de bien-séance, diners nombreux, petits soupers, bals champêtres pour la jeunesse, rien ne manque aux habitans; plusieurs ont des bibliothèques dans leur fermes. Ils cultivent la musique, la littérature et les arts. . . . On se croiroit dans un des pays les plus civilisés de l'Europe."

members, it was easy to keep up the old order, but these instances were few. Great was the need of the new country, where the circumstances of pioneer life and the rapid increase in population rendered the regular administration of church ordinances an impossibility.

Glancing at the church establishments in the older settlements when immigration began, one sees as the leading denominations, the Congregational in New England, the Presbyterian in the Middle group, and the Episcopal in the South. Though the Catholics were to be found in Maryland and the Middle group, generally they had not received the encouragement conducive to the upbuilding of a large, strong church, and in 1790 numbered only thirty-five priests and thirty churches with outlying stations. The Baptists, Methodists, and a variety of other sects were to be found in all of the states at the close of the Revolution; but these denominations ministered to the needs of the poorer members of society, or to a particular nationality, and were looked down upon by the more favored classes. All of the churches suffered to a greater or less degree during the Revolution. The civil-ecclesiastical connection which had existed in Virginia, and to a certain extent in New York and New Jersey, was broken, and voluntary support became a necessary concomitant of church maintenance. The Episcopal church especially suffered through the severing of ties which bound it to Great Britain. The main body of the clergy were Tories, and the end of the war found most of the Virginia parishes without clergymen. As England had been the source of supply, there was an appalling amount of readjustment necessary in order to meet the changed conditions. The Episcopal church was further weakened by the establishment of the Methodist Episcopal Society as a separate organization soon after peace was declared. Religious interests had suffered greatly during the Revolution and the years immediately following. The actual destruction of church property and the languishing condition of many congregations, owing to the loss of preachers and members due to the war and emigration, contributed to this end. In the readjustment attendant upon the Revolution, religious interests were crowded into the background. A spirit of rationalism was plainly manifest in the United States as well as in Great Britian and on the Continent.

It was during this period that churches began to be established west of the mountains. In a region peopled by emigrants from the thirteen states, Great Britain, and the Continent, no uniform religious establishment would be expected. Moreover, an established church required regular support and a trained ministry. These the western country

Religious Conditions Prior to 1800

could not furnish. The emigrants as a body were poor. Rich only in enthusiasm, determination, and physical strength, they were to transform the western country in time; but for the present, wealth lay in the fertile soil, and unremitting labor alone would work the change.

Though Episcopalians, Congregationalists, and Roman Catholics were to be found among the immigrants to the western country, they were greatly outnumbered by other denominations. The disastrous effects of the Revolution upon the Episcopal church rendered it impossible to care for such members as migrated to the West, and these in many instances united with other churches. The Congregationalists as early as 1788 established the town of Marietta on the Ohio and from that date emigrated in increasing numbers to the territory north of the Ohio, especially to the region known as the Western Reserve. During the Revolutionary period several Catholic families had migrated to Kentucky, and the needs of these Kentucky settlers and of the Catholic families in the Mississippi valley, whose residence dated from the French occupation, engaged the attention of Bishop John Carroll who sent Rev. Stephen Badin to minister to them in 1793.

The denominations characterized by wealth and social position did not furnish the majority of the immigrants who poured into the western country at the close of the Revolution. Presbyterians, Baptists, and Methodists were strong in the regions first stirred by the fever of western migration. The religious interests represented in the new country naturally depended, at first, upon the previous church connections of those who had settled in any particular locality. Of the leading denominations the Presbyterian alone had numerous representatives among the immigrants. Strong in the western districts of Pennsylvania and in the back woods of Virginia, its members were among the first to penetrate the wilderness. The Scotch-Irish farming system, which answered well enough so long as the virgin soil would yield its plentiful return of crops, soon exhausted the land. Those practicing this method did not understand or had not the patience to adopt the methods of the "Pennsylvania Dutch" for recuperating land, and the prospect of cheap fresh lands and of larger farms across the "big river" (the Ohio) lured them on.[1] Notwithstanding the bright prospects, healthy climate, and good soil, many settlers became restless and dissatisfied with their location, which they believed inferior to Kentucky. The hardships encountered served to inspire them with the desire for new adventures, although in early times the capture of boats and the destruction of families were frequent.[2]

[1] Joseph Smith, *Old Redstone*, 12.   [2] *Ibid.*, 48.

Religious Conditions Prior to 1800   17

These men and women in many instances carried their religion with them and maintained as far as possible the old faith. Some looked to Scotland for their ministers, and the synod of the Associate Reformed church sent over its missionaries. The presbytery of Old Redstone, embracing southwestern Pennsylvania, and the adjoining regions of Virginia along the Ohio River, furnished many members and preachers for the churches of the wilderness. The ministry that rendered such efficient service beyond the mountains and along the Ohio and its tributaries was trained in its schools. The Presbyterians were among the most influential of the western settlers, a strong contrast to their Baptist neighbors, who rivaled them in numbers, but whose indifference to education gave them a position of less prominence in the new territory. The father of Presbyterianism in Kentucky was Rev. David Rice who moved to Mercer County, Kentucky, from Virginia in 1783. He was also instrumental in organizing the first Presbyterian church in Cincinnati in 1790. In Tennessee, the first Presbyterian immigrant followed the line of the Holston River into eastern Tennessee about 1780 where the Presbyterian church was for many years the leading denomination.

By the year 1800 a number of presbyteries had been organized west of the mountains under the two synods of Virginia and the Carolinas. Under the synod of Virginia there were, in the western part of that state, the presbyteries of Hanover, Lexington, and Winchester. To the north in western Pennsylvania and extending over the settlements west of the Ohio were the presbyteries of Redstone and Ohio, also under the synod of Virginia. This synod likewise included the presbyteries of Washington and West Lexington in Kentucky and the presbytery of Transylvania in western Kentucky and the Cumberland region of Tennessee.[1]

The synod of the Carolinas had under its jurisdiction in western North Carolina, southwestern Virginia, and eastern Tennessee the presbyteries of Orange, Concord, Abingdon, Union, and the short-lived presbytery of Greenville.[2]

Baptists were to be found among the earliest settlers in Kentucky,[3] and Tennessee and the region north of the Ohio River. Thousands of Baptists were among the pioneers in Kentucky and Tennessee, and churches were naturally

[1] For synods and presbyteries, date of constitution, and location see the *Minutes of the General Assembly*, I (1789-1820); Gillett, *History of the Presbyterian Church*, I, II (index); Mss. Minutes of the Presbytery of Transylvania, II.

[2] The presbytery of Greenville, constituted in 1799, was dissolved in 1804 (Gillett, I, 367; II, 201; *Minutes of the General Assembly*, I [1789-1820]).

[3] Squire Boone, brother of Daniel Boone, and several members of the great pioneer's family were Baptists; see Newman, "History of the Baptist Churches in the United States," *American Church History*, II, 333.

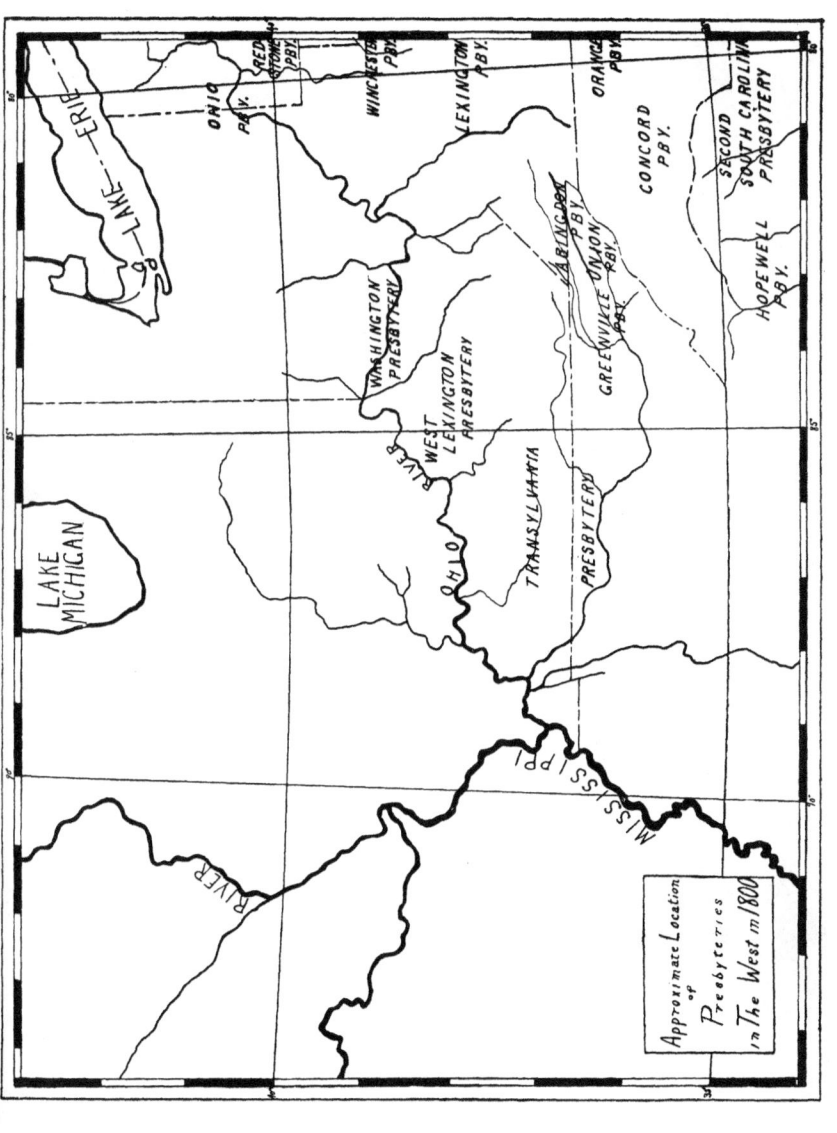

formed wherever Baptists were in reach of one another. Not only were they the first to preach the gospel in Kentucky, but for numbers and influence they held ascendency there for many years.[1] In such numbers did ministers and members of this denomination emigrate from Virginia that many of the old churches were depleted. One historian speaks of Kentucky as the cemetery of Virginia Baptist preachers.[2] "It is questionable with some whether half the preachers who have been raised in Virginia have not emigrated to the western country."[3] By the year 1800, there were 106 Baptist churches with a membership of more than 5,000 in Kentucky alone.[4]

In Tennessee, Baptists were not the first settlers, though tradition points to two Baptist churches constituted in that region before the Revolution.[5] About 1780, a large number of Baptists with eight or ten of their preachers emigrated from Virginia and North Carolina to the Holston country in eastern Tennessee.[6] In the western part of that

[1] Benedict, *A General History of the Baptist Denomination in America*, abridged ed., 811, 812, quoting from an article by Rev. J. M. Peck in *American Quarterly Register* (1841).

[2] Robert B. Semple, *History of the Baptists in Virginia* (ed. 1894) 456, note.

[3] *Ibid.*, 226. [4] Riley, *History of Southern Baptists*, 119.

[5] Benedict, *A General History of the Baptist Denomination in America*, abridged ed., 791.

[6] Newman, *History of the Baptist Churches in the United States*, 336.

territory, though a considerable number of Baptists were to be found among the first settlers, it was not until 1790 that churches were established and the denomination really began to flourish there.[1]

The Baptist churches west of the mountains had organized several associations to unify their work. In western Pennsylvania and the adjacent parts of Virginia and Ohio territory, there was the Redstone Association.[2] The New River Association was made up of the Baptist churches in Virginia west of the Blue Ridge (which had formerly been in the Strawberry Association) and the churches about Greenbrier, later constituted as a separate association.[3] West of the Blue Ridge in North Carolina was the Mountain Association, constituted in 1799 by a division of the Yadkin Association, the churches mainly in North Carolina with a few in Virginia and Tennessee.[4] The churches in Tennessee were grouped under the Holston Association,[5] in the east, and the Mero District Association,[6] in the west. Associations

[1] Benedict, *op. cit.*, II, 219.   [2] *Ibid.*, I, 598.

[3] Greenbrier Association was constituted in 1807; see Robert B. Semple, *History of the Baptists in Virginia* (ed. 1810), 325-27.

[4] Benedict, *A General History of the Baptist Denomination in America*, II, 111, 113; Robert B. Semple, *op. cit.* (ed. 1810), 278, 279.

[5] Benedict, *op. cit.*, II, 215.

[6] Name taken from the name of the civil department which then comprehended all of the counties of western Tennessee; see Benedict, *op. cit.*, II, 219-21.

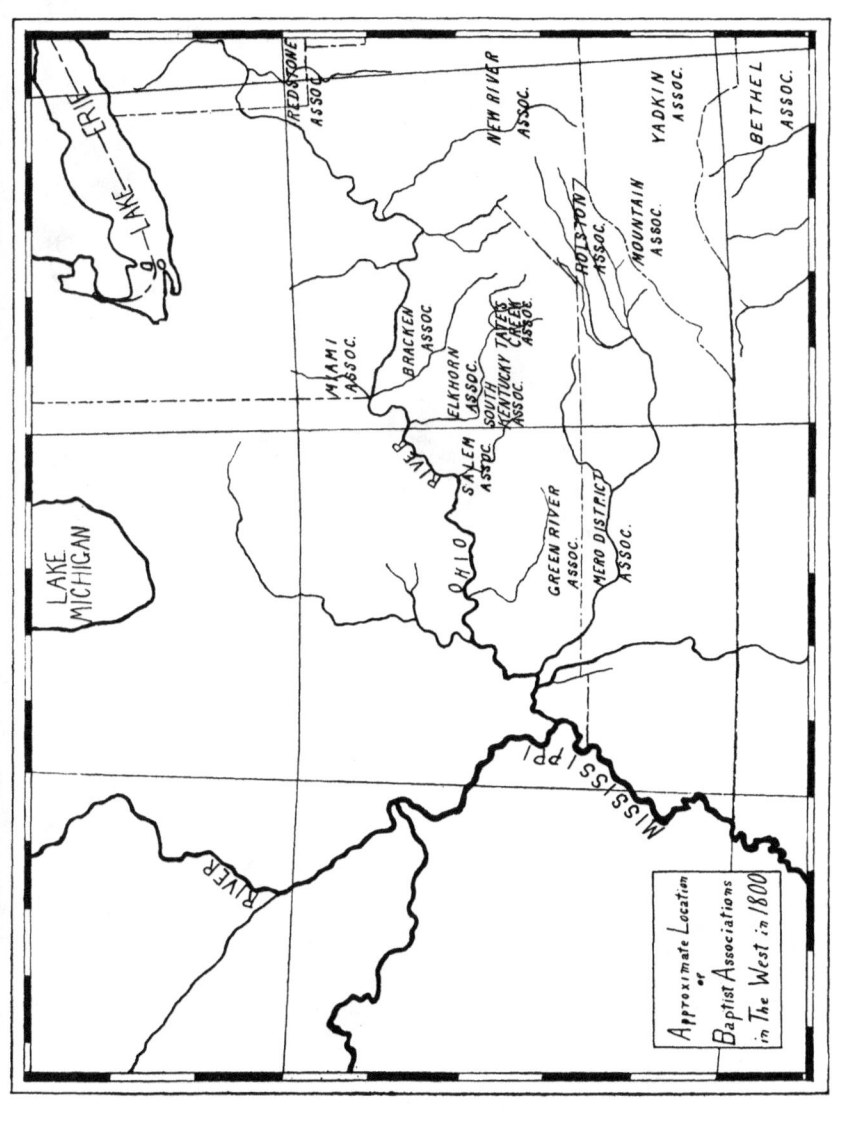

were more numerous in Kentucky than in Tennessee. In the eastern part of the state the churches were associated in the Elkhorn, Bracken, and Tate's Creek associations. The churches in Mason, Bracken, and Fleming counties east of the Licking River separated from the Elkhorn Association in 1798 and formed the Bracken Association. South of the Kentucky River the Separate, or South Kentucky Association was the first established. A part of these churches formed the Tate's Creek Association in 1793.[1] West of the Kentucky River was the Salem Association, composed mainly of churches in Nelson County. In the southwestern part of the state, the Green River Association was formed in 1800, comprising the churches in Logan County. The churches in the Ohio territory between the Miami rivers were included in the Miami Association.[2]

Many Methodist families, too, were numbered among the emigrants from Virginia and North Carolina to the western country. Bishop Asbury early included the remote West in his plan of evangelization.[3] The first Methodist preacher

[1] Benedict, *op. cit.*, II, 229, 235, 236, 242.

[2] *Ibid.*, 242, 244, 258, 259; Dunlevy, *History of Miami Baptist Association.*

[3] *Asbury Journal*, I, (June 11, 1781); I, (June 26, 1782); I, (April 30, 1786); II, (journey to Holston, April 28, 1788); II, (first visit to Kentucky, May, 1790); Lee, *A Short History of the Methodists in the United States*, 84; Atkinson, *Centennial History of American Methodism*, 128, 129.

appointed to the Far West was appointed to the Holston River region in 1783.[1] By the year 1800, as a result of the indefatigable labors of the early itinerants, the Methodist church in Kentucky, Tennessee, and the territory north of the Ohio counted a membership of over 2,700.[2] The societies in this region met at first in two conferences: Holston and Kentucky. Later on one conference was held for the entire region. This conference, called at first the Kentucky Conference, was in the year 1801 organized as the Western Conference.[3] The following circuits made up this conference in the year 1800: Lexington, Danville, Salt River and Shelby, Hinkstone, Limestone, Miami, Scioto, Cumberland, New River, Holston, Russell, and Green.[4]

All of the denominations represented in the West labored under certain disadvantages. It was impossible to supply the demand for ministers, and the church ordinances could not be administered regularly. There were few meeting-houses, even by the end of the eighteenth century. Pro-

[1] *Minutes of the Methodist Conferences*, I, 39 (1783); Stevens, *History of the Methodist Episcopal Church*, II, 93, 132, 337; Atkinson, *op. cit.*, 128.

[2] *Minutes of the Methodist Conferences*, I, 243 (1800).

[3] *Ibid.*, I; *Asbury Journal*, II, 46, 74, 76, 127, 128, 161, 164, 192, 222, 249, 286, 287, 392-94; Burke, *Autobiography*, 55, 57.

[4] Price, *Holston Methodism*, I, 291.

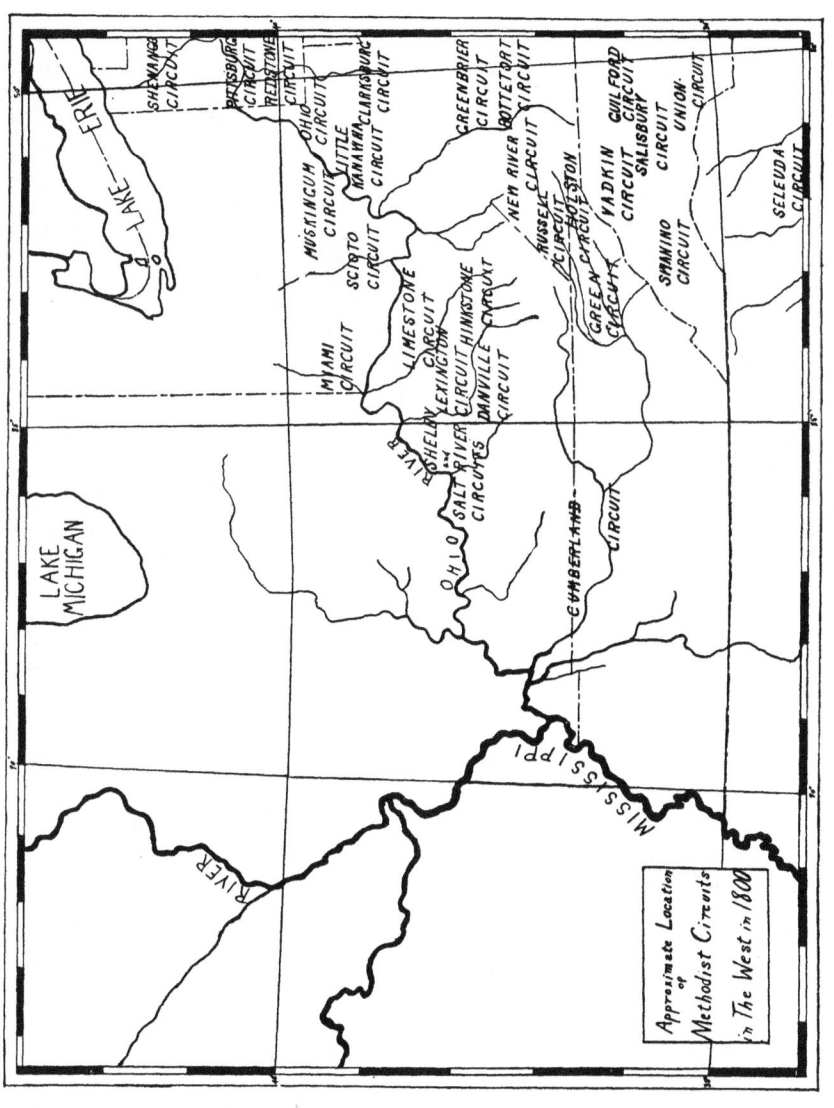

Religious Conditions Prior to 1800

visions for daily needs and the constant watchfulness necessary to preserve life in the presence of a determined foe absorbed the time and thought of the hardy backwoodsman and left little leisure in which to consider matters of general import. The meeting-houses that were erected by the joint labor of those interested were rude structures, similar to the log cabins of the settlement. Services were often held in the open air, in some well-shaded grove, or in one of the more commodious cabins. Congregations were small, ordinarily, and the simple service of prayer, Bible-reading, and singing was conducted by a layman in the absence of a regular preacher. The outlying settlements were rarely visited by ministers of the gospel. The Baptist preacher, mainly dependent upon his own energy for support, necessarily found his interests limited to the church or churches immediately under his charge. The Presbyterian minister, too, usually confined his attention to a certain definite area. It was the Methodist itinerant with his well-nigh indefinite circuit that penetrated the very heart of the wilderness. Wherever he went the gospel was preached, in the cabin, on the roadside, whenever and wherever he could find an opportunity to speak with anyone.

It is evident that the tide of western emigration carried with it many professors of religion more or less attached to some particular denomination.

That the most numerous were Presbyterian, Baptist, and Methodist has been demonstrated. But is evident that religion in the western country it was an infiltration rather than the result of a definitely organized movement. The more earnest of these emigrants sent back reports of the destitute spiritual condition of life in the West, and an effort was made to meet the needs by sending out missionaries. It was customary at first to appoint these missionaries for a short period only—a few months of the year. The provision was most inadequate, as one man devoting all of his time to a given locality would have had under his charge several churches and could have preached only occasionally to each society. But it was difficult to support such missionaries as were sent out, and this partial attention was all that could be expected.

The Presbyterian church devised campaigns of home missionary enterprise in its presbyteries and synods, detailing pastors for temporary mission work among the Scotch-Irish immigrants into the hill-country. The Congregationalists of New England followed with Christian teaching and pastoral care members who moved to western New York and Ohio. In 1801 they united with the General Assembly of the Presbyterian church, the better to carry on the work. By the Plan of Union, as this agreement was called, union churches were to be formed in the new settlements. Resolutions were adopted by the Presbyterian General Assembly and the Congregational General Association of Connecticut to the end that harmony and union might be promoted in the churches in the West. Provision was made for settling any difficulties that might arise, by directing where appeal should be made by members of both denominations.[1]

As early as 1789 the General Assembly of the Presbyterian church decided that each synod should recommend two members well qualified to be employed as missionaries on the frontier.[2] In 1793 the General Assembly employed three missionaries, during the next five years, four or five annually. And for the three years preceding 1802 seven or eight were sent out each year.[3]

The missionary movement in the Baptist church seems to date from the beginning of the nineteenth century. Many ministers of this denomination as well as Presbyterian and Methodist preachers went on their own account into the western country and did much to keep up the interest in the spiritual life, working hard during the week on their farms, and preaching regularly on the Sabbath as well as often during the week.

[1] Kennedy, *The Plan of Union*, 149-51.
[2] *Minutes of the General Assembly*, I, 10, 11.
[3] *Weekly Recorder*, August 16, 1814.

The most indefatigable of the missionaries was the Methodist itinerant. Daunted by no hardship, these strong young men, full of zeal for the salvation of souls, traveled their assigned districts year in and year out, devoting themselves wholly to propagating the gospel. The Methodist itinerant was a familiar figure on all of the highways and could be distinguished as far as the eye could reach. "The grave, earnest countenance, the straight-breasted coat, the oil-skin covering of the hat, the leather saddle-bags, and the staid gait of the horse denoted the Methodist preacher. . . . ." Such was their faithfulness that the saying became almost proverbial of a bitterly cold winter day "There is nothing out today but crows and Methodist preachers."[1] "Their very presence checked levity in all around them."[2]

The meager salary which the churches could afford was wholly inadequate when paid, and often, for lack of funds, could not be collected. In spite, however, of hardships and privations they were happy, as one of their own number testifies: "We were successful and we were happy; we took no thought for the morrow and made no provision for the days to come."[3] Traveling through the

[1] Atkinson, *Centennial History of American Methodism*, 164, 165.

[2] *Biography of Elder Barton W. Stone, Written by Himself*, (ed. 1853), 5.

[3] Atkinson, *op. cit.*, 146 (Rev. Nicholas Snethen).

country, they lodged with the family that chanced to be nearest when night fell, or camped in the woods. Bishop Asbury in his *Journal* has left a fascinating and faithful account of the difficulties attendant upon life in the wilderness. Though they were gladly welcomed by such Methodist families as had migrated to the new country, these, too, were poor and had little to offer save the necessary food and shelter. Here the itinerant was made one of the family, as indeed were all guests at that time when inns were for the most part unknown and every door stood open to strangers.

True to his vocation the itinerant never entered a house without praying with the family, conversing with the members about the welfare of their souls, and instructing the children. From his saddle-bags he brought forth journals and books calculated to minister to the spiritual nature, and these were distributed among the people.

Many of the immigrants were God-fearing men and women, and the missionaries were hailed with joy. Few books[1] found their way over the

[1] Almost the only books besides the spelling-book and primer advertised for sale in the *Lexington Gazette* in 1788 were Watts's *Psalms* and other books of divinity, and English and Dutch Testaments (*Lexington Gazette*, June 28, September 6, 1788). The *Frankfort Palladium* in 1798 advertised "A Summary Declaration of the Faith and Practice of Baptist Church of Christ," and announced that it is suitable to hang upon the wall (*Palladium*, August 9). The same paper on August 14, 1798, adds to its list of books for sale "A Sermon on Sacred Music by

mountains in those days of slender purses and difficult traveling; yet one shelf was provided in many of the cabins for the treasured Bible and hymnal. These books with the *Pilgrim's Progress*, Young's *Night Thoughts*, Doddridge's *Rise and Progress of Religion in the Soul*, Knox's *History of the Church of Scotland*, *The Westminster Confession*, lives and journals of godly men, sermons by eminent divines, and books of kindred character furnished reading for young and old. The fathers and mothers who read books of this description naturally trained their children along the lines suggested, especially in the Book of Books. The serious side of life was held constantly in view, and children in such homes were taught usually by the mother to memorize the Scripture, the catechism, and selected hymns. Family worship was held in great esteem. The preachers laid great stress upon the latter as essential to the well-being of the family. Sin, regeneration, future punishment, and kindred subjects were ordinary topics of conversation, and no pains were spared to make the children conscious of their responsibility for right conduct.

Rev. John P. Campbell." June 20, 1799, one of the Frankfort merchants notified the public that he had purchased "a large and valuable assortment of Books on Law, Physick, Historical Miscellanies and Divinity." He also advertised German Bibles and Watts's *Psalms* and *Hymns* bound together (*Palladium*, June 20, 1799).

Religious Conditions Prior to 1800

Children were made acquainted with the Bible in school as well as at home. It was frequently used as a textbook, of necessity, owing to the scarcity of books. The primers contained selections from the Bible, and it was not unusual to see among the illustrations scenes from the Bible and the *Pilgrim's Progress*, or a picture of the death of some martyred saint. Schools were usually opened with singing and Scripture reading, and prayer was not uncommon. These schools, often in the home of a minister, naturally reflected their surroundings, and were more or less religious as the case might be.

Thus in the frontier settlements spiritual interests were cared for. But by no means all of the immigrants were interested in formal worship, and in many homes there was no pretense of godliness. Bishop Asbury wrote in March, 1797:

I am of the opinion it is as hard or harder for the people of the West to gain religion as any other. When I consider where they came from, where they are, and how they are, and how they are called to go farther, their being unsettled with so many objects to take their attention, with the health and good air they enjoy, and when I reflect that not one in a hundred came here to get religion; but rather to get plenty of good land, I think it will be well if some or many do not eventually lose their souls.[1]

There was good ground for the complaint of immorality, gambling, and intemperance so frequently found in the comments on western life

[1] *Asbury, Journal*, II, 286.

of the period. Many of the immigrants were men and women with no sense of moral responsibility. Criminals of all descriptions sought the new country where it was necessarily difficult to administer the law. Hard drinking and rough and degrading amusements formed the only recreation of the lower classes of society, and the lawless life of this element stamped many localities with a low moral tone.

During the closing years of the eighteenth century there was a marked decline in church membership throughout the country. Indeed, since the Revolution there had been an increasing apathy and coldness in the American churches generally, which had filled the leaders with apprehension and alarm. Here and there an occasional revival in one or another denomination as among the Presbyterians in western Pennsylvania (1781-87), the intermittent revivals among the Methodists, confined to no particular locality, and among the Baptists and Presbyterians in Virginia during the years 1785-92, had served to quicken the declining interest; but so general was the depression by the end of the century that it was a subject of earnest concern to all Protestants.

A variety of causes contributed to this decline. The unsettled state due to the Revolution had necessitated careful attention to the things of the present world rather than preparation for the

Religious Conditions Prior to 1800

world to come. Disaffection with the new government and its methods of procedure furnished abundant material for conversation and action. Ardent sympathizers as many of the Americans were with the French Revolution and the spirit that lay behind it, they could not but be influenced by the doctrines so freely circulated which led to the overthrow of the conventional in religious as in political life. The new settlements to the west of the mountains, too, had drawn an ever-increasing number of immigrants, especially after Wayne's victory ended the fear of Indian aggressions, and many became indifferent to religion in a country where there were so few facilities for public worship. Thus church membership east of the mountains decreased with no corresponding increase in the West. The supply of ministers was affected by the inability of societies to support a pastor, or even contribute a fair share toward his support, forcing those who might otherwise have chosen the ministry to seek other means of livelihood. The Revolution had interfered with the work carried on by the English societies for the Promotion of Christian Knowledge and for the Propagation of the Gospel which had ministered to the needs of the English settlers in America. Disaffection, too, in denominational ranks, as that of O'Kelly in the Methodist church, decreased the membership.[1]

[1] Bennett, *Methodism in Virginia*, 313-31.

The churches generally bemoaned this spirit of decline and sought to revive the interest in religion. About 1796, Christians of different denominations in Europe and America united in a quarterly concert of prayer for the revival of religion in the world and for the more general propagation of the gospel.[1] In the Presbyterian church, the year 1796 was marked beyond all others by official calls to fasting and prayer by presbyteries, synods, and the General Assembly for the outpouring of the Holy Spirit. A large number of congregations in western Pennsylvania had drawn up written covenants to pray for a revival.[2] Bishop Asbury made the following note in his *Journal*, February 27, 1795:

> Mr. Wesley lived to see two general revivals of religion, one at the beginning, the other about thirty-six years ago; though, doubtless, they had generally a gradual growth of religion: we also have had two revivals—one at the beginning, the other about seven years ago: the third revival has now taken place in England, and I hope ours will soon follow.[3]

Revivals had from the first been an important feature in the work of the Methodists, and continual efforts were made by bishops and preachers to stimulate such meetings. Though no special

---

[1] Stillman, *Discourse before the Massachusetts Missionary Society* (1803), 5.

[2] McDonnold, *History of the Cumberland Presbyterian Church*, 10, 11.

[3] *Asbury, Journal*, II, 217.

effort is recorded of the Methodists at the close of the century, it is but natural to suppose that the decreasing membership was a subject of anxiety and earnest prayer. Anxiety manifested itself in the increased solemnity of religious meetings and the oft-repeated question, "What shall I do to be saved?" The interest in this important question of salvation bore fruit in the great religious revival that swept over the United States in the closing years of the eighteenth and the first years of the nineteenth century. This revival in the West was of a peculiarly interesting character and merits closer attention. The next chapters will deal with the leaders of the movement and the means used to promote the revival.

CHAPTER II

THE REVIVAL LEADERS: THEIR TEACHINGS AND METHODS

The Great Revival at the end of the eighteenth century, so widespread and far-reaching in its results, began simultaneously in different parts of the country and in different denominations. Reports of the period from New England furnish evidence of a quickened interest in religious affairs among Congregationalists in many towns of Massachusetts and Connecticut, and also in the more newly settled regions of New England and western New York, where missionaries from the older communities were laboring. In the Methodist church in the East, particularly in Delaware and Maryland, Bishop Asbury in his *Journal* records revivals. West of the mountains, where the excitement reached its height, its first appearance was in the Cumberland region in Kentucky and Tennessee among the Presbyterians. Most peculiar bodily exercises[1] marked this revival in the western country which soon affected Baptists and Methodists as well as Presbyterians.

In the interval that had elapsed between the founding of the first churches in the wilderness and

[1] These will be treated in detail in chap. iv.

The Revival Leaders

the Great Revival of 1800, the unknown West had become an important part of the Union. The rapid increase in population had its advantages and its disadvantages. The horizon was immensely widened; but there was a restlessness born of the constant shifting of newcomers, an uncontrolled sense of freedom, and an aggressive spirit manifest in all the new communities. Weighty questions, commercial and political, of the relations existing between these communities and the government east of the mountains, threatened at various times to disturb the peace. The immigrants, representing a great variety of social, political, and religious opinions, naturally differed often upon the essential as well as the minor questions at issue in the society they formed.

In the churches, the heated controversies over points of doctrine had engendered a spirit in the professors of religion that greatly troubled the really devout. To the eager young preachers who had migrated to the West in large numbers during the last decade of the eighteenth century, the want of spiritual aggressiveness was a matter of serious import. They viewed with grave apprehension the worldly interests of many professing Christians and their purely formal interest in matters pertaining to religion. To these men the western country was the abode of every wickedness, and the picture presented was gloomy indeed. Impressed with the need of reform, they labored diligently to preach the gospel, to awaken the people to the sinfulness of careless indifference to their own spiritual welfare and that of their neighbors. The people in the remote settlements of Kentucky and Tennessee were earliest impressed by the need of improvement along the lines suggested. A large number of local preachers of the Methodist denomination and several Presbyterian preachers and lay members of both denominations had moved to that region about 1798. Many of these immigrants had come from churches which had been profoundly shaken by revivals, and they were eager to further such movements in the new country. Fear was aroused by impassioned preaching. The question of salvation became to many the all-important topic of conversation. The apprehensive spirit which this fostered gave an increased solemnity to all religious gatherings.

The notion that salvation must be experienced in some unmistakable manner gave rise to a feverish excitement that later generations realize was bound to find violent expression because of its intensity. Conversion was a very serious affair. The throes of the new birth were often protracted for weeks and months before the hope of salvation brought relief to the sufferer. No pains were spared to make plain the necessity of this salvation. The joys of heaven were pictured in most

The Revival Leaders

alluring colors, the voice of the preacher, modulated to suit the theme, changed perceptibly as he strove to rouse in his audience a desire to participate in this everlasting joy. Small wonder that his listeners cowered before him when in an equally effective manner he dwelt upon the torments of hell.

The origin of the Great Revival which so powerfully stimulated religious enterprise all over the United States at the beginning of the nineteenth century is best understood by a study of the men who roused the indifferent Christians from their lethargy and directed the revival which ensued. These leaders were earnest, enthusiastic young men whom no hardship could daunt. Day after day they labored to break the shell of lifeless formality which incased the majority of professing Christians and to reach the young people and those who made no pretense to orthodox Christianity.

The central figure was a minister of the Presbyterian church, James McGready. Of Scotch-Irish parentage, James McGready was born in Pennsylvania about 1760.[1] His parents moved to Guilford County, North Carolina, where his boyhood and early youth were passed in such labor

[1] Joseph Smith (*Old Redstone*, 361) notes that he was about thirty years of age when licensed to preach (1788); James Smith (*History of the Christian Church*, 561) gives the date of his birth as 1763; birthplace, North Carolina.

as persons of no very extensive property were accustomed to perform in those years in the Carolinas. In speaking of his early days he said that he never omitted prayer from the time he was seven, did not drink, swear, break the Sabbath, or indulge in other excesses. Such were his sedateness and punctuality in religious duties and desire for religious improvement that an uncle took him to western Pennsylvania to educate him for the ministry and placed him under one of the leading Presbyterian preachers. Fully persuaded in his own mind as to his sanctification, he was shocked one day when he was about twenty years old on overhearing a conversation between two of his friends in regard to his spiritual condition. This led him to examine himself carefully and he found the new spiritual life they had declared he lacked. On August 13, 1788, he was licensed by the presbytery of Redstone, and, after supplying for a time, obtained leave to travel in the Carolinas during the winter. On his way, he passed through places in Virginia that had recently been visited by a revival, and stayed some time at Hampden-Sidney College.[1]

In North Carolina, McGready found religion at a low ebb, and did all in his power to better conditions. Whenever he preached, the excitement was great, and an extensive revival soon

[1] Joseph Smith, *Old Redstone*, 360–64.

The Revival Leaders

spread over Orange and some of the adjoining counties. Barton W. Stone, another of the revival leaders, thus describes him:

> His person was not prepossessing, nor his appearance interesting, except his remarkable gravity, and small piercing eyes. His coarse, tremulous voice excited in me the idea of something unearthly. His gestures were *sui generis*, the perfect reverse of elegance. Everything appeared by him forgotten but the salvation of souls. Such earnestness, such zeal, such powerful persuasion . . . . I had never before witnessed.[1]

Such was the excitement caused by his work in South Carolina that fierce opposition was aroused. He was accused of "running people distracted" and of diverting them from their necessary vocations. The opposition went so far as to tear away and burn his pulpit and send him a threatening letter written in blood. This opposition led to his removal to the West in 1796.[2] After spending several months in eastern Tennessee, he accepted a call from some of his former hearers who had settled in the southern part of Kentucky. Here in Logan County he became the pastor of three churches: Gasper River, Muddy River, and Red River. His diligent efforts to promote a revival were rewarded. The effect of his impassioned preaching and conscientious pastoral work was

[1] Stone, *Biography*, 6, 7; see Appendix I for Ninian Edwards' opinion of McGready.

[2] James Smith, *History of the Christian Church*, 562–64.

soon visible. Within a year there were signs of the Great Revival that was to sweep over the western and southern states. He drew up a solemn covenant[1] which bound all who signed it to offer special prayer every Saturday evening, Sunday morning, and the third Saturday of each month for one year for the outpouring of the Holy Spirit in Logan County, Kentucky, and throughout the world.

The period of quickened interest in 1797 was followed in the autumn by a general deadness which continued until the following July. In that month

[1] "When we consider the word and promises of a compassionate God, to the poor lost family of Adam, we find the strongest encouragement for Christians to pray in faith—to ask in the name of Jesus for the conversion of their fellow-men. None ever went to Christ, when on earth, with the case of their friends that were denied, and although the days of his humiliation are ended, yet for the encouragement of his people, he has left it on record, that when two or three agree upon earth, to ask in prayer, *believing*, it shall be done. Again *whatsoever ye shall ask the Father in my name that will I do, that the Father may be glorified in the Son*. With these promises before us we feel encouraged to unite our supplications to a prayer-hearing God, for the out-pouring of his spirit, that his people may be quickened and comforted, and that our children, and sinners generally, may be converted. Therefore we bind ourselves to observe the third Saturday of each month, for one year, as a day of fasting and prayer, for the conversion of sinners in Logan County, and throughout the world. We also engage to spend one-half hour every Saturday evening, beginning at the setting of the sun, and one-half hour every Sabbath morning, at the rising of the sun, in pleading with God to revive his work."—James Smith, *op. cit.*, 565–66.

The Revival Leaders

a sacramental meeting was held at Gasper River and most of the families in the neighborhood "became impressed with a sense of their ruined condition." In September of that year, McGready's two other congregations experienced a quickened interest in spiritual affairs. This, too, was succeeded by a period of apathy owing to the ridicule of Rev. James Balch, a Presbyterian minister who traveled through the Cumberland region in a spirit of opposition to the methods employed by McGready. In the summer of 1799, however, the excitement was renewed,[1] and the movement soon assumed proportions that amazed even those most interested.

Prominent among the promoters of this Great Revival were the two brothers John and William McGee, the former a Methodist, the latter a Presbyterian preacher. Both had received the careful religious training that Presbyterian parentage implied in those days, and the younger son, William, entered the ministry of that denomination. John McGee, while in Maryland, became a Methodist. He returned to his home in Guilford County, North Carolina, the country of McGready's boyhood and the scene of his later labors, to take up the work of the ministry as a local preacher, and labored in the revival which began in that county. In 1798 he moved to the

[1] James Smith, *op. cit.*, 566–68.

West and settled in Sumner County, Tennessee, where his brother William had already settled.[1]

Other prominent Presbyterian leaders were William Hodge, Barton W. Stone, John Rankin, and Robert Marshall. William Hodge, who had been one of the revival preachers in North Carolina, and a friend of McGready's, settled in Sumner County, Tennessee, the year before William McGee moved there. Barton W. Stone, also from the same region in North Carolina as McGready and the McGee brothers, settled in Bourbon County, Kentucky, and became the pastor of two congregations there. He and Robert Marshall, who moved to Kentucky in 1793 and became the pastor of Bethel and Blue Spring churches in eastern Kentucky, were fellow-laborers in the revival, and both left the Presbyterian church as a result of the revival, having become convinced of error in its doctrine.[2]

In the Methodist denomination the revival owed much to the labors of William Burke and William McKendree. William Burke, an elder, and one of the ablest Methodist itinerants, labored in the western territory on different circuits from the

[1] Mss Minutes of Transylvania Presbytery, II, 108: "Paris, October 4, 1796, Rev. Wm. McGee from Orange Presbytery, N. Carolina, appearing in Presbytery and expressing a wish to become a member, Presbytery . . . . admitted him a member"; *ibid.*, 110: McGee was called by the Shiloh congregation.

[2] Marshall returned to the Presbyterian church in 1810.

The Revival Leaders

year 1792. The preceding year he had attended a Methodist quarterly meeting and experienced conversion. Describing his conversion, he relates that he fell senseless to the floor and knew nothing until he found himself on his feet giving glory to God. In 1795, the year in which he was ordained an elder, he was appointed to the Mero district in Tennessee. In 1796 he was transferred to the Guilford district in North Carolina, and the year following returned to the Holston circuit in eastern Tennessee. The year 1798 found him again itinerating in the Cumberland River region, and in the year 1799 he was sent to the Danville circuit. After attending the General Conference at Baltimore in 1800, he returned to the Hinkstone circuit in Kentucky. At Bishop Asbury's request he was to have general oversight of the church interests in that region.[1] William McKendree, who became a bishop in the Methodist church, figures most prominently in the history of western Methodism. He was born in Virginia in 1757. His parents were worthy pious people in moderate circumstances. During the Revolution, he served his country faithfully. About 1787, he joined the Methodist church and labored several years in Virginia and South Carolina. The revival had already begun in Kentucky when he was appointed

[1] Burke, *Autobiography*, found in Finley, *Sketches of Western Methodism*.

in 1800 to the Kentucky Conference as the western conference was then called. His first year was very successful, and his indefatigable energy did much to spread the revival.

Prominent among the Baptist preachers in the West at the end of the century were the two brothers Louis and Elijah Craig, both from Virginia. Louis Craig had been one of the leading Baptist preachers in Virginia and had suffered much persecution at the hands of the enemies of that denomination. He moved west in 1781 and finally settled in Bracken County, Kentucky. He excelled in exhortation and could often move an audience that other preachers had failed to reach. John Taylor, Ambrose Dudley, Moses Bledsoe, and William Hickman also labored in the western country and did much to promote and carry on the Great Revival among the Baptists.

Before entering more fully upon a discussion of the revival movement, it will be well to consider the truths taught by these revival leaders, and the methods by which the movement, once begun, was carried from one region to another. The men who promoted the revival and with whom it gained favor as the excitement increased were marked by a fervid, impressive manner of preaching. Of one of these, Rev. William McGee, it is related that "he would sometimes exhort after the sermon, standing on the floor, or sitting, or lying in the dust, his eyes streaming, and his heart so full that he could only ejaculate, 'Jesus, Jesus!' "[1] McGready pictured the delights of heaven and the terrors of hell in a peculiarly realistic manner.[2] An extract from one of his sermons on the text, "The fool hath said in his heart, there is no God," well illustrates this:

The Character, History and End of the Fool.—He died accursed of God when his soul was separated from his body and the black flaming vultures of hell began to encircle him on every side. Then all the horrid crimes of his past life stared him in his face in all their glowing colors; then the remembrance of misimproved sermons and sacramental occasion flashed like streams of forked lightening through his tortured soul; then the reflection that he had slighted the mercy and blood of the Son of God—that he had despised and rejected him—was like a poisoned arrow piercing his heart. When the fiends of hell dragged him into the eternal

[1] Davidson, *History of the Presbyterian Church in Kentucky*, 263.

[2] F. M. Davenport, *Primitive Traits in Religious Revivals*, 67: "His doctrine was a modified Calvinism. He dwelt upon the necessity for the new birth and the importance of knowing the time when and the place where the conversion had occurred. This was a new note in the Presbyterian denomination in that section of the world. But there was another note in the gamut of his eloquence that was not new. In New England under Edwards, and in Old England under Wesley, it had sounded forth clear and strong and terrible in fearful denunciation of the wrath of God upon impenitent sinners. A friend of McGready (Rev. William Barnett) said of him that he would so array hell before the wicked that they would tremble and quake, imagining a lake of fire and brimstone yawning to overwhelm them and the hand of the Almighty thrusting them down the horrible abyss."

gulf, he roared and screamed and yelled like a devil. When, while Indians, Pagans, and Mohammedans stood amazed and upbraided him, falling like Lucifer, from the meridian blaze of the Gospel and the threshold of heaven, sinking into the liquid, boiling waves of hell, and accursed sinners of Tyre and Sidon and Sodom and Gomorrah sprang to the right and left and made way for him to pass them and fall lower down even to the deepest cavern in the flaming abyss. Here his consciousness like a never-dying worm stings him and forever gnaws his soul; and the slighted blood of the Son of God communicates ten thousand hells in one! Now through the blazing flames of hell he sees that heaven he has lost—that exceeding great and eternal weight of glory he has sold for the devil's pottage! In those pure regions he sees his father, or mother, his sisters, or brothers, or those persons who sat under the same means of grace with him, and whom he derided as fools, fanatics, and hypocrites. They are far beyond the impassable gulf; they shine brighter than the sun when he shineth in his strength and walk the golden streets of the New Jerusalem; but he is lost and damned forever.

The last thing we shall mention in the history of the fool is when he lifted up his eyes in hell, he found a dictionary, explaining the meaning of all the profane language he used during his life. Now he perfectly understands the meaning of those words he was in the habit of using in this world without ever reflecting on their signification. Such expressions as the following were very common with the fool in this life: "I'll be damned, God damn his soul, if it were not so." Now the fool perfectly understands the meaning of these terms in all their horrid emphasis—for God has heard and answered his prayer: he has damned his soul in hell. He could now tell you that the dreadful meaning of these words frighted the stoutest devils, and fills all the flaming vaults of hell with the most hideous shrieks and yells. In this life when the fool was offended with any one his common phrase was such a one is a damned fool. Now he perfectly understands the meaning of the phrase. When he surveys his life and reflects on the many offers of salvation he refused; the manner in which he misspent his precious time and misimproved all the means of grace; he is constrained to confess he is emphatically a fool—a damned fool—for he is damned in hell forever and ever.[1]

No imagery was too vivid to illustrate the theme. With powerful energy the revival preacher reiterated the doctrine of salvation through the blood of Jesus Christ. The sinner, and in this category all were included, could not hope for salvation by his own efforts, the "Blood of the Lamb" alone could save him. The Calvinistic doctrines of predestination and regeneration clashed with the Arminian doctrine of salvation for all, which the Methodists preached with great fervor and which became the leading tenet of the Great Revival of 1800.

This Great Revival was the result of a combination of causes, some clearly defined and others so interwoven with the general history of the period that it is impossible to catch more than a suggestion of their outlines. The Great Revival was not the result of a carefully planned campaign on the part of any denomination or denominations. Yet there were certain phases in different parts of the

[1] McGready, *Posthumous Works*, I, 228, 229.

country in those regions where the movement was simultaneous that suggest the working of general principles, even where the work was carried on by different denominations.

In order to understand its development, some knowledge of the denominational life of the churches chiefly affected by it is necessary. Among the Presbyterians who laid great stress upon an educated ministry there was in the religious services an intellectual atmosphere quite apart from everyday life. The stiff, technical theology, or dry, speculative orthodoxy of the pulpit made but little impression on the heart and conscience of those addressed. It was a rare thing for young people to approach the communion table, as age and experience seemed necessary to an understanding of the confession required of those who wished to unite with the church, and there was nothing to attract the young. The Baptists went to the extreme in the West in their opposition to education, holding that it impaired rather than augmented the ability of a would-be pastor. Fierce persecution in Virginia and other states had engendered a hatred of the established clergy and everything savoring of episcopacy that was well-nigh fanatical. Clinging tenaciously to the principle that it was better for the pastor to earn his own living, they furnished meager support for their ministry. In the West, particularly, where so much effort was required to make suitable provision for a growing family, the Baptist pastor had little time for books, even if he had had the inclination to study. The Methodist society from its inception had laid great stress upon personal religion. When, shortly after the Revolution, the Episcopal church in America lost many of its members by the formal coming out of the Methodists and their establishment as a separate ecclesiastical body under the superintendence of Bishops Coke and Asbury, it lost a most active, earnest band of workers. They were poor people it is true, and despised by society at large, yet they were men and women filled with a sense of the necessity of correlating in some measure profession and life. To the Methodist, religion was something to be actually experienced and felt, and the emotions played a large part in his worship. The class-meeting, organized early in the movement, has been of great importance in the history of the church. Here were to be found earnest men and women, usually not more than twelve, whose formal religious needs were met by the established church, but who desired a more complete knowledge of the way of salvation. Regular meetings were held, under one of their number who had been appointed leader for prayer, praise, exhortation, and consultation. The leader kept in closest touch with the members of his class, and, after the church was fully organized, made regular reports to the preacher and deacon concerning the spiritual condition of those under his charge and concerning the funds collected.

Class-meetings were promptly organized by members of the society who migrated to the West, the most efficient of their number acting as leaders. Thus a vital connection was maintained between the different members of the church in this meeting where all phases of the religious life were carefully discussed. Absences were inquired into, and only good and sufficient reasons excused the delinquent, who might be dropped from the class-list if the excuse were not satisfactory. In this way the Methodist church maintained a more careful supervision of its members than the other denominations. The itinerant system was especially adapted to the needs of a new and sparsely settled country. The faithful circuit riders rendered most efficient service. Few of them had thought of the ministry as a calling until inspired at some Methodist meeting to give up their regular mode of life and travel about the country to present the truth which had so powerfully impressed them. They were for the most part uneducated, ignorant in many instances of all books save the Bible and the hymnal. Many of them thought, as did the Baptists, that learning was a hindrance, but their leading men favored education and even erected a college in Abingdon,

Maryland, called after the founder Cokesbury. The opposition, for a time, however, gained the ascendency, as the early educational ventures failed owing to fire and mismanagement.

In the western country, a friendly feeling among the Presbyterians, Methodists, and Baptists was much in evidence in spite of doctrinal differences. The exigencies of life in the wilderness drew them together, and it was not uncommon to find the various denominations uniting in their larger meetings, though the Baptists did not mingle as freely as the others. It is not surprising to find the Great Revival movement animating them all at the same period. Certain general characteristics are to be noted in all the denominations affected by the revival. A period of indifference on the part of professing Christians to spiritual concerns was generally followed by a time of feverish anxiety, marked by increasing solemnity in all religious gatherings, which resulted in periods of revival often characterized by wildest excitement. This was the effect of the impassioned preaching, earnest exhortation, loud prayers, and energetic singing.[1] Protracted meetings which grew out of the reluctance on the part of those most seriously impressed to leave the scene of worship as the work progressed became a regular feature of worship and were instrumental in promoting the revival.

[1] See Appendix II for one of the favorite hymns.

Sacramental occasions and quarterly meetings afforded the best opportunity for reaching the people generally. These were usually well attended, even before the Great Revival, as they furnished an opportunity of meeting friends and hearing the gospel to many who in their remote cabins knew no neighborhood life and were out of reach of even the irregular preaching afforded by most western communities at the end of the eighteenth century. The sacramental meetings were a great feature in such lives. This the revival leaders were quick to appreciate and take advantage of. As soon as it became noised about that unusual excitement was to be found at these meetings, great crowds flocked to them. The increased attendance made it necessary to devise some new scheme of entertaining those who came from a distance, since the hospitality afforded by the neighborhood was no longer adequate. This resulted in the development of camp-meetings, which immediately became an important element in religious life and most effectively fostered the revival spirit.

Just when and where the camp-meeting originated is a disputed question. In the early days of the Revolution, the Baptists in Virginia had held meetings similar in some respects; but at these meetings men only had remained on the

The Revival Leaders

grounds over night.[1] As early as 1794, one of the Methodist churches in Lincoln County, North Carolina, decided to hold a meeting in the neighboring forest for several days and nights. This meeting was conducted by several ministers, among whom was William McKendree, later prominent in the Great Revival in the West. So successful was the plan that another meeting was appointed for the next year, and still another for the year following. These meetings were kept up continuously in the South Carolina Conference.[2] Since several of those who were instrumental in promoting the Great Revival in the Cumberland region of Kentucky and Tennessee had come from the Carolinas, where these meetings were well known, it might naturally be inferred that they had brought the plan with them. There is, however, no evidence that such meetings were even attempted in Kentucky or Tennessee before the year 1800. Furthermore, Bishop Asbury who traveled at regular intervals over all the circuits does not use the word camp-meetings in his *Journal*

[1] Robert B. Semple, *History of the Baptists in Virginia*, 23; Benedict, *A General History of the Baptist Denomination in America*, II, 395–97 (so-called camp-meetings were also instituted a few years later by John Waller in his endeavor to build up a strong party to support his independent views).

[2] Atkinson, *Centennial History of American Methodism*, 489, 490.

until the year 1802. Jesse Lee in his history of the Methodists states that the camp-meeting was introduced about the year 1801. He adds, "I never could learn whether they began in the upper parts of South-Carolina, in Tennessee, or in Kentucky."[1]

In the Great Revival of 1800, the necessity for camping on the ground at the large meetings was first made evident in the Cumberland region where the revival originated. It was impossible to provide entertainment for those who lived too far from the grounds to return home at night. Then, too, as the excitement increased, the night meetings became a most important feature of the gatherings, and the people were loath to leave the place at all. Those coming from a distance drove, if possible, to the place of meetings, and it was a simple matter for them to come ready to camp for several days. To men and women who had once made the difficult journey over the mountains there was no novelty in the idea of camping out. The warm summer and autumn nights could easily be spent out of doors with such shelter as the wagon or an improvised tent furnished. The scheme was first adopted in McGready's congregations in Logan County, Kentucky. The great meeting at Red River in the summer of 1800 made it imperative

[1] Lee, *A Short History of the Methodists in the United States*, 279.

The Revival Leaders

to provide in some way for the throngs likely to attend subsequent meetings. At the Gasper River meeting the last Sabbath in July of the same year, thirteen wagons were brought to the meeting-house to transport people and their provisions. In August a meeting was held at Muddy River. "There were twenty-two wagons loaded with people and their provisions; with many others provided for encamping at the meeting-house."[1] Thus the plan of camping on the ground immediately gained favor, and people were advised to come prepared to remain on the ground, if they desired to attend all of the meetings and if they lived too far to return home at night. In eastern Kentucky the same necessity, crowded meetings in sparsely settled communities, favored the adoption of the scheme of camping on the ground, already familiar in the western part of the state. Soon camp-meetings came to be a regular feature of the revival and were to be met with wherever it spread. These meetings usually began on Thursday, or Friday, and continued until the following Tuesday. People living thirty, sixty, and even one hundred miles away attended. There was preaching every day with the administration of the Holy Sacrament on Sunday. Provisions and bedding were brought from home by those who

[1] "McGready's Narrative of the Revival in Logan County," *New York Missionary Magazine* (1803), 192, 196.

purposed remaining on the ground. The wagons were stationed at a convenient distance, near wood and water. Improvised tents and rude huts, hastily constructed, supplemented the covered wagons and afforded the necessary shelter. The numbers attending increased to such an extent that the meeting-house could not accommodate the crowds, and stands were erected in the grove near by in order that several ministers might preach at the same time. As the excitement increased, the singing, praying, and exhortation were kept up in various parts of the grounds night and day. There was no regularity about the life. Many seemed unconscious of the need of food and sleep.[1]

To appreciate the part which the camp-meeting played in the Great Revival of 1800, it is advisable to look more closely at the scenes enacted at such meetings. The meeting at Gasper River, in July, 1800, probably the first of the camp-meetings, may be taken as a typical instance of the earliest gatherings of this sort.

On Saturday evening, after the congregation was dismissed, a few seriously exercised Christians were sitting conversing together, and appeared to be more than commonly engaged, the flame started from them and appeared to overspread the whole house. The greater part of the ministers and several hundreds of the people remained at

[1] Ramsay, *History of South Carolina*, II, 32–37, note on camp meetings.

the meeting-house all night. Through every part of the multitude there could be found some awakened souls, struggling in the pangs of the new birth, ready to faint or die for Christ, almost upon the brink of desperation. Others again . . . . beginning to tell the sweet wonders which they saw in Christ. Ministers and experienced Christians were everywhere engaged praying, exhorting, conversing, and trying to lead enquiring souls to the Lord Jesus. In this exercise the night was spent till near the break of day.

Toward the close of the sermon on Sunday, "the cries of the distressed" arose almost as loud as the voice of the preacher.

No person seemed to wish to go home—hunger and sleep seemed to affect nobody—eternal things were the vast concern. Here awakening and converting work was to be found in every part of the multitude. . . . . Sober professors, who had been communicants for many years, now lying prostrate on the ground, crying out: "I have been a sober professor; I have been a communicant; O! I have been deceived, I have no religion—Oh! I see that religion is a sensible thing. . . . . Believe what the ministers tell you—religion is a sensible thing. . . . . I feel the pains of hell in my soul and body! O! how I would have despised any person a few days ago who would have acted as I am doing now!—But O! I cannot help it!

And this continued till deliverance came.

Little children, young men and women, and old gray headed people, persons of every description, white and black, were to be found in every part of the multitude . . . . crying out for mercy in the most extreme distress.[1]

[1] "McGready's Narrative of the Revival in Logan County," *New York Missionary Magazine* (1803), 192–94.

The following extract from a letter written by a gentleman in North Carolina in July, 1802,[1] gives a good picture of the more developed camp-meetings.

The preparatory service was to commence on Friday. On the evening before, however, the camps began to be pitched in the wilderness, and not within the view of any artificial improvements of any kind.

I attended as an astonished spectator. The great and wonderful works which appeared . . . . are as far above my powers of explanation as of comprehension. Near 200 heavy wagons were upon the ground besides other carriages, and it is thought there could not be less than 5,000 persons. Two stands were erected on the grounds and at a convenient distance for the daily exhibitions of the public speakers and also a table for administering the Lord's Supper. The stands were occupied by different ministers, while the Lord's Supper was administering to perhaps about 700 communicants.

The camp was well illuminated through the night by a good fire being kept up in front of every camp, besides candles which were kept burning in different parts of the encampment. The whole of the time was taken up both day and night (time for every necessary refreshment only excepted) in praising, praying, preaching and exhortation . . . . divine service was constantly kept up, perhaps the whole of the time both day and night.

Professing ministers of the gospel of different sects attended, viz., of the Presbyterian, Methodist, and Baptist churches and performed their respective duties occasionally with very great zeal and fervency, night and day, as their respective abilities enabled them to undergo the extraordinary fatigue.

[1] *New York Missionary Magazine* (1802), 310-12.

The Revival Leaders

A very great number of people of every age, I believe from 10 years to 70, were struck down. To risk a conjecture of the precise number would be idly uncertain because they fell in the camps, on their way home, and after they got there. The whole number who fell must have amounted to many hundred. It was thought that more than two hundred were down at one time. Many were exercised with very great apparent severity, and the time of continuation was very different upon different subjects. Some appeared to be exceedingly distressed and considerably exercised, who were not struck down, but walked to their tents with the assistance of one or two persons, where, after lying a few hours, they became comforted and composed in a tolerable degree, and some of them in a very extraordinary degree.

They were struck down and exercised in many different ways, although they generally trembled exceedingly, and were remarkably cold in their bodily extremities. After they recovered, some said they felt a great load about their heart, a little before the severity of the stroke; others said they were rather in a slumbering and inattentive way, not at all affected at that moment, with what they were hearing or had heard, when they were struck down in an instant as with a thunderbolt.

Some were totally insensible of everything that passed for some considerable time, others said they were perfectly sensible of every word spoken in their hearing, and everything done to them although to the spectator they appeared in a state of equal insensibility. Many cried out exceedingly when they were first struck down; their cries were like those of the greatest bodily distress imaginable. But this was generally succeeded, in a little time, by a state of apparent insensibility which generally lasted much longer; and which, in some, was succeeded by the strongest appearance of extreme agitation and distress exhibited by incessant cries for mercy, and acknowledgements of unworthiness and ingratitude to a blessed Savior.

The people did not fall so much immediately under the ministry as they did at their camps, or walking through the space between the different encampments, and when not in hearing of the public speakers.[1]

Another eyewitness thus describes the meetings:

At first appearance those meetings exhibited nothing to the spectator but a scene of confusion, that could scarce be put into human language. They were generally opened with a sermon; near the close of which there would be an unusual outcry; some bursting forth into loud ejaculations of prayer, or thanksgiving for the truth: Others breaking out into emphatic sentences of exhortation: Others flying to their careless friends, with tears of compassion beseeching them to turn to the Lord. Some struck with terror, and hastening through the crowd to make their escape, or pulling away their relations.—Others, trembling, weeping and crying out for the Lord Jesus to have mercy upon them; fainting and swooning away 'till every appearance of life was gone. . . . . Others surrounding them with melodious songs or fervent prayers for their happy resurrection in the love of Christ. . . . . Others collecting into circles around the variegated scene, contending with arguments for and against. And under such appearances the work would continue for days and nights[2] together.[3]

[1] See Appendix III for a letter written July 7, 1802, describing a camp-meeting in the district of Spartenburgh, South Carolina (*Augusta Herald*, July 28, 1802).

[2] The scene at night was peculiarly impressive. Torches, candles, and the blazing camp-fires among the trees threw a weird light upon the moving crowd, the animated preacher, the agonized sufferer, and the prostrate bodies. Under these circumstances there was something truly awful in the medley of sounds that fell upon the ear.

[3] McNemar, *The Kentucky Revival*, 23.

So popular did the method of encamping on the ground at the large meetings become that it was soon adopted by the leaders as a means of stimulating revivals.[1]

Praying societies played a most important part in the spread of the revival. McGready writes: "Was I to mention the rapid progress of its work, in vacant congregations, carried on by means of a few supplies, and by praying societies . . . . it would be more than time or the bounds of a letter would permit of."[2] A special gift of prayer is frequently mentioned as attending the revival movement. Thus by prayer, exhortation, and religious conversation in private as well as through the regular channels of public worship the Great Revival movement gradually spread over the whole of the western country. The spread of this Great Revival and its culmination will form the subject of the next chapter.

[1] The subsequent development of the camp-meeting and its later importance will be treated in chap. v.

[2] Letter in *New York Missionary Magazine* (1802), 160.

CHAPTER III

THE SPREAD OF THE REVIVAL AND ITS CULMINATION

As already stated in the preceding chapter, the Great Revival in the West at the end of the eighteenth century began in the Cumberland River region in Logan County, Kentucky. The determined efforts of the Presbyterian preacher, James McGready, so stimulated the congregations to which he ministered that a revival resulted as early as the year 1797. In the month of May, "a woman who had been a professor in full communion with the church found her old hope false and delusive—she was struck with deep conviction and in a few days was filled with joy and peace in believing. She immediately visited her friends and relatives from house to house, and warned them of their danger in a most solemn, faithful manner, and plead with them to repent and seek religion," thereby awakening many.[1] The awakening became more general in 1798. A solemn sacramental meeting in July of that year filled the minds of those who attended with the profound claims of immortality. Secular business seemed forgotten.

[1] McGready letter, October 23, 1801, in *New York Missionary Magazine* (1802), 156.

Men under deep conviction spent the days alone in the woods weeping and praying. Groups met in the houses and talked of eternity and wept over their ruined condition. To most of these, deliverance was delayed. In 1799, the interest was still deeper, and more burdened souls found salvation.[1]

In July of that year, the sacrament of the Lord's Supper was administered at Red River. "On Monday the solemnity was very great during the time of preaching; many of the most bold, daring sinners of the country were brought to cover their faces and weep bitterly." The people, most of whom lingered about after dismissal, were collected in the meeting-house for prayer. "It appeared evident that the power of God filled the house— Christians were filled with joy and peace in believing, and sinners were powerfully alarmed under an apprehension of the horrors of an unconverted state." A few weeks later, the fourth Sabbath in August, McGready assisted at a meeting at Gasper River, which charge he had resigned to John Rankin. Here "many persons were so struck with deep heart-piercing convictions that their bodily strength was quite overcome so that they fell to the ground and could not refrain from bitter groans and outcries for mercy." McGready overheard

[1] McDonnold, *History of the Cumberland Presbyterian Church*, 11, 12; James Smith, *History of the Christian Church*, 564-69.

a man say to his wife and children: "Alas! we have been blind all our days—we are all going to Hell together—Oh! we must seek religion, we must get an interest in Christ or to Hell we must go." He wrote of the poor giddy young people, who, on the first days of the solemnity, could not behave with common decency, lying prostrate on the ground, weeping, praying, and crying for mercy. "In the space of three weeks after above twenty of those awakened gave the most clear satisfying accounts of their views of the glory and fulness of the Mediator." The meeting at Muddy River in September surpassed all previous gatherings. In October the sacrament was administered at the Ridge (a vacant congregation in western Tennessee), by McGready, McGee, and Rankin, and the revival spread to that region. The winter of 1799 was for the most part a "time of weeping and mourning with the children of God."

During the summer of 1800, the revival assumed such proportions that McGready wrote that all before was as a few scattering drops before a mighty rain. A meeting was held at Red River in June of that year.[1] The account of this meeting as given by John McGee is of value as the account of an eyewitness and participator in the scenes

[1] "McGready's Narrative of the Great Revival in Logan County," *New York Missionary Magazine* (1803), 152–54.

Spread and Culmination of Revival 65

described.[1] A number of Presbyterian preachers, McGready, Hodge, Rankin, and others, attended and so effectively did they preach that "many felt the force of the truth and tears ran down their cheeks." On Monday, the last day of the feast, as Mr. Hodge was preaching, a woman lost all self-control and shouted for some time, finally sitting down in silence.

Some of the Presbyterian preachers left the meeting-house after the services were over to consult about certain matters. The McGee brothers remained with the people, many of whom were weeping and who seemed loath to leave their seats. William McGee, overcome by his feelings, sank unconscious upon the floor of the pulpit. John was seized with violent trembling and could not preach as he desired. Finally he arose and told the people there was a greater than himself present and urged them to submit that their souls might live. At this many gave vent to their feelings in words, and a woman, the same who had shouted under Mr. Hodge's preaching earlier in the day,

---

[1] Redford, *History of Methodism in Kentucky*, I, 268–70. (This letter was written from memory in 1820. McDonnold, *History of the Cumberland Presbyterian Church*, points out the probable inaccuracy of McGee's date of 1799: "He describes even events which seem to belong to the next year." A letter written by John McGee, dated Tennessee Settlement, Cumberland, October 27, 1800, refers to what is probably the same meeting [*Extracts of Letters*, 4–6].)

"shouted tremendously." John McGee left the pulpit to quiet her, for he feared the effect of such loss of self-control upon the Presbyterians who were not accustomed to disorder in their meetings and might object to the confusion. The excitement, however, was too intense for him to withstand, and, feeling that it was "the work of God," he threw himself heartily into it, "shouting and exhorting with all possible energy." The result was that many literally fell to the floor, where they lay, some joining in the cries for mercy which resounded on all sides, others perfectly helpless. This strange scene filled the Presbyterian ministers with amazement when they returned to the usually quiet meeting-house. McGready estimated that ten people were converted on this occasion.

The news of the unusual happenings at the meeting was spread broadcast by the four or five hundred people present. Naturally this resulted in an increased desire on all sides to attend the sacramental meetings in order to witness the novel excitement. The Red River meeting was followed by others in quick succession at Gasper River, Muddy River, and other places in that section of the country. So intense had the excitement become that people planning to attend were advised to bring provisions with them and come prepared to camp on the ground if they desired to remain throughout the meetings. In August of the same year (1800), a large number attended the Methodist Quarterly meeting "at Edward's chapel on the Cumberland side of the Ridge," and the Friday following, another sacramental meeting was held at the Ridge, ten miles distant. John McGee describes the latter as the "most glorious meeting that my eyes ever beheld." It continued four days and nights, during which, from the best accounts which we have collected since, there were more than one hundred souls converted to God. "It was truly affecting to hear the groans of the spiritually wounded intermingled with the shouts of heaven-born souls." Two weeks later at a meeting on Blidsoe's Creek in western Tennessee there was great opposition from old professors and deists: "nevertheless the Lord worked like himself in power. Sinners were cut to the heart and falling to the ground cried for mercy . . . . then rising gave glory to God with loud voice." Probably sixty or seventy people were converted at this meeting.[1] The same writer speaks of the meeting a short time after on Desha's Creek as "perhaps the greatest meeting we ever witnessed in this country."[2]

To follow the Great Revival as it spread over Kentucky and Tennessee, into North and South

[1] Letter from John McGee, dated Tennessee, Settlement of Cumberland, October 27, 1800, in *Extracts of Letters Containing Some Account of the Work of God since 1800*, 4-6.

[2] McGee, letter written in 1820; Redford, *History of Methodism in Kentucky*, I, 271.

Carolina, western Virginia, western Pennsylvania, and the regions north of the Ohio River in detail is not necessary. The same phenomena of bodily exercises amazed each new community that witnessed them and stamped the work with a peculiar character unknown to the more regularly conducted revival meetings of the same period in New England and in the East generally.

Several of the younger members of a Presbyterian congregation in Sumner County, Tennessee, were present at the meeting in July, 1800, at Gasper River. The very evening they reached home they held a meeting which lasted all night. The next day the neighborhood came together for prayer. Some fell and were unable to rise until assured of regeneration. By the next Sabbath, about twenty persons, mostly orderly and accepted church members of several years' standing, experienced a "change of heart." Thus the work was carried from one locality to another and soon spread over western Tennessee. In eastern Tennessee the same lack of interest in spiritual matters seems to have preceded the revival. A Presbyterian preacher wrote that his ministrations in Blount County, Tennessee, were attended with the least success in the years 1798 and 1799. A striking change appeared about the end of March or the first of April, 1800. Religion became more the topic of conversation than usual, and more at-

Spread and Culmination of Revival 69

tention was paid to preaching. A greater seriousness and solemnity were visible, and several began to be much impressed. The sacrament was administered in May. The Monday services were marked by especial interest. A society for prayer and religious conversation was instituted, and a monthly lecture for children was appointed. Stimulated by the reports of revivals in other places, the movement steadily progressed, marked, however, with little enthusiasm or extravagance.[1] In localities similar to the one just described where unusual seriousness prevailed, the presence of those who had witnessed the excitement attending the revival farther west usually served to introduce the peculiar phenomena characteristic of the work there. One locality after another was affected, and the revival became general in eastern Tennessee.

In considering the revival movement in the eastern part of Kentucky, it is important to note the converging of simultaneous movements among the Baptists, Methodists, and Presbyterians. These separate movements were given a special impetus by the revival in the southwestern part of the state, and a mighty revival followed in the year 1801.

[1] See in *New York Missionary Magazine* (1801), 237-40, a letter from Gideon Blackburn dated Blount County, eastern Tennessee, September 29, 1800: "The ministers and well wishers of Zion in this remote branch of the vineyard of Christ were almost ready to cry out 'Has God forgotten to be gracious?'"

70   The Great Revival in the West

The revival among the Baptists began in Boone County in the year 1799.[1] The Elkhorn Association, which included the churches where the revival originated, reported, August 8, 1801, a gain of 3,011 members by baptisms in one year.[2] In the Methodist societies throughout the country a new zeal was manifested after the General Conference held in Baltimore in the month of May,

[1] Benedict, *A General History of the Baptist Denomination in America*, II, 251: "This great revival in Kentucky began in Boone County on the Ohio River, and in its progress extended up the Ohio, Licking, and Kentucky rivers, branching out into the settlements adjoining them. It spread fast in different directions, and in a short time almost every part of the state was affected by its influence. It was computed that about ten thousand were baptized and added to the Baptist churches in the course of two or three years."

[2] Letter from Rev. Dr. Rogers dated Philadelphia, November 2 (1801), to a friend in Baltimore: "The printed minutes of Elkhorn Baptist Association, held in Kentucky, August 8, 1801, were put into my hands . . . . last Friday, by which it appears that the said Association consists of 36 churches, 10 of which had applied at the time above for admission, and were accepted. The addition to this Association had been in one year only by Baptism, 3,011. Four of the churches had received by baptism 1,378 members: between 300 and 400 severally; viz., Great Crossings Church . . . . 376, Bryant's, 367, Clear Creek, 326, South Elkhorn, 309. Some had received the same year between 2 and 300, others between 1 and 200; in some under 100, down to 30, 20, 10, 8, and 6 persons. There are several other associations in that state. . . . . I am most credibly informed that upwards of 10,000, at the lowest calculation, had been baptized in one year only, preceding the above period" (March, *Increase of Piety, Or the Revival of Religion in the United States of America*, 59).

Spread and Culmination of Revival 71

1800. This conference surpassed its predecessors in animated preaching and the number of conversions. Elders and preachers returned to their respective fields of labor fired with a desire to promote revivals. A number of preachers from eastern Kentucky attended this conference and undoubtedly did much to prepare that region for the great excitement which raged in 1801 and the years immediately following. A Presbyterian clergyman, Rev. George Baxter, president of Washington Academy at Lexington, Virginia, wrote of eastern Kentucky:

In the older settlement of Kentucky, the revival made its first appearance among the Presbyterians, last spring [1801]. The whole of that country about a year before was remarkable for vice and dissipation, and I have been credibly informed that a decided majority of the people were professed infidels. During the last winter, appearances were favorable among Baptists and great numbers were added to their churches. Early in the spring the ministrations of the Presbyterian clergy began to be better attended than they had been for many years before; their worshiping assemblies became more solemn; and the people after they were dismissed showed a strange reluctance at leaving the place. They generally continued some time in the meetinghouses in singing or in religious conversation. Perhaps about the last of May or the first of June, the awakening became general in some congregations and spread through the country in every direction with amazing rapidity. I left that country about the 1st. of November, at which time this revival, in connection with the one in Cumberland, had covered the whole State, excepting a small settlement which borders on the waters of Green River, in which no Presbyterian ministers are settled and I believe very few of any denomination. The power with which this revival has spread and its influence in moralizing the people are difficult for you to conceive and more difficult for me to describe. I had heard many accounts and seen many letters respecting it before I went to that country; but my expectations though greatly raised were much below the reality of the work.[1]

Reports of the meetings in Logan County spread all through the country, and people traveled for a long distance to see for themselves what was going on. Barton W. Stone, pastor of the Presbyterian societies at Concord and Cain Ridge, Bourbon County, Kentucky, distressed at the formal state of religion in his congregations and hearing of the great work in southwestern Kentucky under the ministry of men he had known in North Carolina, went in the spring of 1801 to investigate the excitement. He returned full of enthusiasm and heartily in sympathy with the work. At Cain Ridge many had gathered to hear his report of the revival in the West and were deeply affected by it. He preached the same evening at Concord and two little girls "were struck down under the preaching of the Word, and in every respect were exercised as those were in the south of Kentucky." Rising,

[1] Letter from Rev. George Baxter to Rev. A. Alexander, January 1, 1802 (Gallaher, *The Western Sketch Book*, 38-49; also given in Price, *Holston Methodism*, I, 343-51).

they addressed the congregation as was customary in such cases. Their words made a deep impression on those present. The excitement was even greater in Mr. Stone's other congregation at Cain Ridge. He found on returning the next day that his report of what he had witnessed in southern Kentucky had stirred the people deeply. As he approached the gate of the house where he was to conduct services he was met by one of his parishioners who shouted aloud the praises of God and rushed into his embrace. The noise attracted the crowd in the house which soon gathered about them. "In less than twenty minutes scores had fallen to the ground. Paleness, trembling, and anxiety appeared in all; some attempted to fly from the scene panic-stricken, but they either fell or returned immediately to the crowd, as unable to get away. The meeting lasted on the spot until late at night, and many found peace in glorification of the Lord."[1] Special excitement was manifested in Mason County among the Presbyterians in April, 1801. At a sacramental meeting near Flemingsburg, the last Sunday of that month, there was "much weeping, trembling, and convulsion of soul." Two little girls, nine or ten years old, cried out in great distress during the meeting and continued praying and crying for mercy till one of them received hope.

[1] Autobiography of Elder Barton W. Stone (Rogers, *The Cane Ridge Meeting-House*, 153–57).

She turned to the other and cried, "O! you little sinner, come to Christ!—take hold of his promises! —trust in him!—he is able to save to the uttermost!—O! I have found peace to my soul! O! the precious Savior! come just as you are, he will take away the stony heart and give you a heart of flesh! you can't make yourself any better.— Just give up your heart to Christ now! You are not a greater sinner than me! You need not wait another moment!" Thus she continued exhorting until the other child "received a ray from heaven that produced a sudden and sensible change; then rising with her in her arms, she cried out in a most affecting manner—'O! here is another star of light!'"[1] The next Sunday about twenty were struck in a meeting at Cabin Creek. Nine out of fifty were "struck down" while worshiping at Cain Ridge.

By the first of June, 1801, such crowds attended the sacramental meeting at Concord that it was necessary to administer the Lord's Supper in a tent erected in a neighboring grove. About 4,000 people were present at this meeting. Two hundred and fifty of these communed. An eyewitness reports that "twelve wagons had brought some of the people with their provisions, etc., from distant places." He continues: "This was the first occasion that showed the necessity of encamp-

[1] McNemar, *The Kentucky Revival*, 21.

Spread and Culmination of Revival 75

ing on the ground, the neighborhood not being able to furnish strangers with accommodation; nor had they a wish to separate."[1]

A gentleman, in a letter dated Lexington, Kentucky, August 10, 1801, wrote: "Last Sunday the Association was held at Higby's, 6 miles from here, where it is said there were from 8 to 10 thousand persons; and on the same day in the two counties adjoining, there were at two congregations, from 18 to 25 thousand souls."[2]

It seems to be generally agreed that the unusual excitement reached its height at the great sacramental meeting held at Cain Ridge in August, 1801. Some estimate the number in attendance as high as 25,000. Allowing for exaggerations, it is certain that thousands attended.[3] A series of smaller meetings had preceded this great gathering,

[1] Letter from Colonel Patterson, Lexington, Kentucky, September, 25, 1801, in *New York Missionary Magazine* (1802), 119; see Appendix IV for Rev. John Lyle's account of sacramental meetings at Point Pleasant and Lexington in June, 1801.

[2] March, *Increase of Piety, Or the Revival of Religion in the United States of America*, 59.

[3] The following extract from a letter dated Bourbon County, August 7, 1801, is interesting: "I am on my way to one of the greatest meetings of the kind perhaps ever known: it is on a sacramental occasion. Religion has got to such a height here, that people attend from a great distance; on this occasion I doubt not but there will be 10,000 people and perhaps 500 waggons. The people encamp on the ground and continue praising God day and night, for one whole week before they break up" (*ibid.*, 56).

and people came from all parts of Kentucky, from Tennessee, and from the territory north of the Ohio. This was a union meeting of Presbyterians and Methodists, and had been published throughout the length and breadth of the country to begin the Friday preceding the third Sunday in August. Thursday and Friday of the week appointed the roads approaching Cain Ridge were filled with wagons and carriages, with men and women on horseback and walking. Services began in the meeting-house on Friday, and lasted until Wednesday evening without intermission. The crowds could not be accommodated within doors, and repaired to a stand erected in the woods. To an onlooker the scene presented the greatest confusion—six or seven ministers preaching at the same time, the crowd shifting as one lifted his voice higher than the other, or otherwise engaged their attention.

A gentleman writing from Lexington, Kentucky, to his sister in Philadelphia, August 10, 1801, thus describes the meeting:

I am sure the most discerning and observant pensman, or the nicest pencil, could not puortray to your imagination, the full idea of the meeting that took place at Kainridge in Bourbon-county:—This meeting was published about one month generally, throughout the Presbyterian connexion as one of their annual sacraments; thither assembled the religious of every denomination, some from 100 miles distant, but more particularly the Presbyterians and Methodists, who are in full communion with each other:—lastly the Baptists, who preach with each other but do not commune. To this general assembly, I set off last Friday and arrived there on Saturday about 10 o'clock: I then began to note some of the most extraordinary particulars: I first proceeded to count the waggons containing families, with their provisions, camp equipage, &c, to the number of 147. At 11 o'clock the quantity of ground occupied by horses, waggons, etc, was about the same size as the square between Market, Chestnut, Second and Third streets of Philadelphia. . . . . There was at this place a stage erected in the woods about 100 yards from the meeting-house, where were a number of Presbyterian and Methodist ministers; one of the former preaching to as many as could get near enough to hear—in the house also was another of the same denomination, preaching to a crowded audience—at the same time another large concourse of people collected about 100 yards in an east direction from the meeting-house, hearing a Methodist speaker—and about 150 yards in a fourth course from the house an assembly of black people, hearing the exhortation of the blacks, some of whom appeared deeply convicted and others converted. The number of communicants who received tokens were 750, nor was there a sufficiency of them—(these tokens are small pieces of lead the size of a five-penny bit with the letter A or B impressed thereon and distributed by the ministers to the members of the several churches not excluding any Baptists who apply for them). I believe there was at one time as many as 300 who exhorted on this occasion. I noted a remarkable instance of a little girl, by the name of Barbara, about 7 years old, who was set upon a man's shoulder, agreeably to her desire to speak to the multitude, which she did until she appeared almost exhausted, and leaned back her head on her bearer. A tender hearted old man standing close behind her, observed,

"Poor thing she had better be laid down"; at which she quickly turned round her head, and said, "Don't call me poor, for Christ is my brother, God my father, and I have a kingdom to inherit, therefore don't call me poor, for I am rich in the blood of the Lamb."[1]

[1] March, *Increase of Piety*, etc., 57, 58. Another description of the same meeting, found in a pamphlet in the Durrett Collection, entitled *Account of an Extraordinary Revival of Religion in Kentucky*, is given in a letter dated Lexington, Kentucky, August 16, 1801 (no other title and no signature; the opening sentences of this letter suggest the letter just quoted from *Increase of Piety*, etc., 57, 58): "There were four large collections hearing preaching (on Saturday at noon) while I believe, nearly as large a number were collected in different little collections praying for those that the power of God had struck lifeless, singing and exhorting notwithstanding it was requested by the Ministers, that no exercises should be carried on during sermons; yet there was singing in one part of the camp without intermission from the time I first arrived until I left the place which was Tuesday ten o'clock containing a term of seventy-two hours. . . . .

"I suppose I saw as many as 800 that were struck down mostly in the following manner: they say they feel very weak in their knees and a want of breath, gaping to gain their breath as one in the agony of death, and instantly fall and lay insensible from 15 minutes to 6, 8, or 10 hours. Some are cramped in the extremities. The first words generally spoken by them after their recovery is, Lord, have mercy, increasing from words to sentences, to exhortations to believe in Christ, to cease to do evil and learn to do well, to depend wholly in the Righteousness of Christ, Their exhortations are accompanied with instant power to the hearts of their hearers." (Children on men's shoulders speaking with power never before heard of—gives instance of little girl just quoted above in the text, senseless two hours, then from a man's shoulder "delivered, it was supposed the greatest body of divinity ever pronounced by human lips." As she finished speaking "don't call me poor &c," a great number fell to the earth

Spread and Culmination of Revival 79

Another eyewitness wrote to a friend:

I attended with 18 Presbyterian ministers; and Baptist and Methodist preachers, I do not know how many; all being either preaching or exhorting the distressed with more harmony than could be expected. The governor of our State was with us and encouraging the work. The number of the people computed from 10 to 21,000 and the communicants 828. The whole people serious, all the conversation was of a religious nature, or calling in question the divinity of the work. Great numbers were on the ground from Friday until the Thursday following, night and day without intermission, engaged in some religious act of worship. They are commonly collected in small circles of 10 or 12, close adjoining another circle and all engaged in singing Watts's and Hart's hymns; and then a minister steps upon a stump or log, and begins an exhortation or sermon, when, as many as can hear collect around him. On Sabbath night I saw above 100 candles burning at once and I saw I suppose 100 persons at once on the ground crying for mercy, of all ages from 8 to 60 years. Some I had satisfaction in conversing with, others I had none; and this was the case with my Brethren as some of them told me. When a person is struck down he is carried by others out of the congregation, when some minister converses with, and prays for him; afterwards a few gather around and sing a hymn

at the sound of her words and glorified God.) The writer had attributed the falling to sympathy, weakness, design, and fanaticism, "but on seeing some fall with their faces covered in the mud, among the horse's heels, apparently dead for a considerable time, then come to pray and exhort without ceasing; some fall . . . . in their shops, or at their plows, having none present to work upon their passions," came to the conclusion that the work was supernatural. See Appendix V for Rev. Mr. Lyle's description of this great camp-meeting.

suitable to his case. The whole number brought to the ground, under convictions, were about 1,000, not less. The sensible, the weak, etc, learned and unlearned, the rich and poor, are the subjects of it.[1]

One of the Methodist preachers records that not being invited to speak he mounted a fallen tree and, shaded by an umbrella, began reading a hymn in an audible voice. A vast crowd soon gathered about him and so the work went on until his voice could no longer be heard, because of the groans and shouts. Hundreds fell prostrate under his preaching as they were doing all over the grounds. McNemar wrote: "The various operations and exercises . . . . were indescribable. The falling exercise was the most noted. James Crawford, one of the oldest ministers in the state, and one of the foremost in the work, informed me that he kept as accurate an account as he could of the number that fell on the occasion and computed it to be about three thousand. The vast numbers who received light on this occasion, and went forth in every direction to spread it render it impossible to pursue any further the particular track of its progress."[2] Another eyewitness describes the scene as awful beyond description. The noise of

[1] See in *New York Missionary Magazine* (1802) a letter from a Presbyterian minister in Kentucky, dated September 20, 1801; also in March, *Increase of Piety*, etc., 85–87. The writer was Rev. John Evans Finley (*ibid.*, 91).

[2] McNemar, *The Kentucky Revival*, 26.

Spread and Culmination of Revival 81

the vast crowd sounded like the roar of Niagara. A strange supernatural power seemed to pervade the entire mass of mind there collected. At one time he saw at least 500 swept down in a moment as if a battery of 1,000 guns had been opened upon them, and then immediately followed shrieks and shouts that rent the very heavens.[1] The impressions made upon the thousands of people who attended can well be imagined.

As suggested by McNemar, it is difficult to pursue the progress of the revival after this meeting, so widespread did the movement become. Naturally the report of the revival in southwestern Kentucky and Cumberland made a deep impression upon that part of the Carolinas which had furnished many of the settlers for that particular region of the West and which had at one time been the home of the very men most active in promoting the revival. Many earnestly desired that the same scenes might be enacted among them. Special meetings had for some time been held in various localities to pray for an outpouring of the Spirit.[2] In August, 1801, at a Presbyterian sacramental meeting held at Cross Roads Church in Orange County, the services had been of an

[1] *Autobiography of Rev. James B. Finley*, 172, 173.

[2] See Appendix VI for an interesting and detailed account of the revival among the Baptists in the Kehukee Association, North Carolina.

unusually interesting character. But the pastor was greatly distressed as he rose to dismiss the services that the meeting was about to close without any special interest. He tried to give utterance to his feelings, "but, overcome with emotion he sat down without uttering a word .... manifest emotion pervaded the congregation. He rose again, but still unable to speak he stood silent. .... At that moment a young man from Tennessee who had been in the Great Revival, raising both hands with a loud voice, exclaimed, 'Stand still and see the salvation of God.'" Intense excitement instantly thrilled the congregation and a large number fell in every direction as if by an electric shock.[1] A Kentucky gentleman wrote to his brother-in-law that the work was still spreading farther through Kentucky and also continued very powerful in the state of Tennessee. "We have late accounts also of a gracious and powerful work in North Carolina of which hundreds have already been made the happy subjects. It began there near about the same time it began in Kentucky."[2] Toward the close of 1800 the revival made a sudden and unexpected appearance among the Baptists in the Sandy Creek Association, attended by most of the new and unusual appearances already assumed in many

[1] Anderson, *Life of Rev. George Donnell*, 63, 64.
New York Missionary Magazine (1802), 128.

Spread and Culmination of Revival 83

places.[1] Among the Methodists, too, the revival movement progressed, and Bishop Asbury makes frequent mention of the work in the Carolinas and Georgia during the early years of the nineteenth century.

In western Pennsylvania toward the close of the eighteenth century there was an indication of special concern in religious matters. Letters from that region speak of religion as being in a more flourishing condition in the winter of 1798–99 than for some years previous. Young people especially were affected.[2] In a letter dated Ten Mile, Pennsylvania, March 9, 1803, it is stated that the revival began among Presbyterians in the Ohio presbytery in August or September, 1802, and had by that time spread into almost all of their congregations. The movement which originated in southwestern Kentucky had spread through the eastern part of the state and along the Ohio River and gave its peculiar stamp to the revival which had already begun in western Pennsylvania, especially along the headwaters of the Ohio River.

Something similar to what you have heard of in Kentucky and the Carolinas has taken place in our neighborhood. A few weeks ago the most remarkable revival of religion ever known in this country made its appearance

[1] Benedict, *A General History of the Baptist Denomination in America*, II, 109, 110.

[2] *New York Missionary Magazine* (1800), 38–44.

here. It first began at the sacrament of the Rev. M'C—15 miles from this place and it is spreading rapidly in every direction. On the Sabbath and Monday after the sacrament not less than 50 were sometimes lying at once crying for mercy, complaining of the hardness of their heart and pleading for pardon. They met every day or night and frequently on both, all that week.[1]

In the year 1801 the excitement pervaded the territory north of the Ohio River. Many from the settlements there had attended the great meetings held in the spring and summer in Kentucky. Presbyterians, Baptists, and Methodists felt the influence of the revival movement. Camp-meetings played here, as elsewhere, a most important part in the movement. Ministers from Kentucky crossed the river and did all in their power to further the revival. By 1803, the excitement had reached the Western Reserve. Rev. Joseph Badger, the missionary sent out by the Connecticut Missionary Society, describes the same protracted meetings, deep solemnity, anxiety concerning salvation, and bodily exercises already noted as characteristic of the revival in Kentucky and Tennessee. The Plan of Union agreed upon by the Congregational General Association of Connecticut and the General Assembly of the Presbyterian church in the year 1801 had drawn the members of the Presbyterian and Congrega-

[1] (Eyewitnesses report one-half not told) *New York Missionary Magazine* (1802), 48.

Spread and Culmination of Revival 85

tional churches in the new settlements in western Pennsylvania and Ohio into close relationship. The first church organized on the Western Reserve was at Austinburg in October, 1801. The membership numbered sixteen.[1] The region was but sparsely settled at that time. In 1803, the same missionary records an increase of bodily exercises with increased seriousness. Some opposed to the work had said that New England people, meaning Massachusetts and Connecticut people, would never become subject to the falling. The facts, however, were such as to alarm opposers. Some who thought themselves proof against the power which brought down those reared in ignorance began to think they were in danger.[2]

By the year 1803 the revival movements in the United States had become so general as practically to cover the territory of the Union. In May, 1802, Bishop Asbury wrote in his *Journal*, "I have a variety of letters conveying the pleasing intelligence of the work of God in every state, district, and most of the circuits in the Union."[3] The report of the General Assembly of the Presbyterian church for 1803 states that revivals more or less general had taken place in the northern and eastern presbyteries. These revivals were not, however,

[1] Letter from Joseph Badger in *American Pioneer*, II, 276.
[2] *Memoir of Rev. Joseph Badger*, 64, 65.
[3] Asbury, *Journal*, III, 63.

marked by the extraordinary exercises which characterized the more extensive revivals in the southern and western presbyteries. Up to the year 1803, the revival continued with practically unabated zeal. In that year, unmistakable signs of declining interest appeared, though the excitement did not lessen much until 1805. Sporadic revivals continued after the latter date in various localities for several years, but the movement was no longer general.

Before discussing the results of this Great Revival, the phenomena of the bodily exercises which gave a peculiar character to the excitement will be considered in their various phases.

CHAPTER IV

PHENOMENA OF THE REVIVAL

Reference has often been made in the preceding pages to the remarkable bodily exercises which accompanied the revival in the West. These exercises played such a prominent part in the revival that a detailed study of the muscular movements themselves and of the mental condition which induced them can alone render the Great Revival intelligible. For intensity and variety and the astonishing ease and rapidity with which they were communicated (affecting at times an entire congregation) these exercises were remarkable. Men, women, and children, professing Christians and pronounced scoffers, the strong and the weak, the educated and the ignorant, were alike affected. Ministers in the pulpit as well as lay members succumbed. Some of those affected were frequently subject to the exercises as long as they lived. No particular place was the scene of operation—the meeting-house, the cabin, the field, the roadside, the school were alike favorable. Given a certain stimulus the individual was seized with one or another form of exercise, whether alone or in company.[1] Friends would gather around the one affected and pray and sing until the patient became normal again. These exercises were usually of short duration, though they sometimes lasted for hours and even for days at a time. One of the Presbyterian ministers wrote to a friend: "The bodily exercise has assumed such a variety of shapes as to render it a truly Herculean task to give an intelligent statement of it to any person who has never seen it."[2] The most frequent forms were falling to the ground, jerking, barking, and dancing. These well merit closer investigation.

The falling exercise was the first to attract attention. As the name suggests, the one affected fell to the ground. To the Methodists there was nothing unfamiliar in the sight, for they had been accustomed to seeing people sink to the floor and lose consciousness under preaching, and instances were on record where entire congregations had fallen. In the revival of 1800 falling became so common that it caused little or no interruption to the service, save as it became necessary to remove

---

[1] "On sacramental occasions they most generally get struck as well as at society. At home families have been wholly taken down. They have fallen on the roadside, plowing in the field, in bed asleep and awake, individually, in family, children at school where no religious exercises were going on" (*Draper MSS*, "The Patterson Papers," No. 105; [see Appendix VII for this letter]).

[2] Gallaher, *The Western Sketch Book*, 53.

those who fell to a place of safety where they would not be trampled upon.[1] The first instances of falling in connection with this revival were reported in a Presbyterian congregation at Gasper River, Kentucky. The climax was reached at the great Cain Ridge meeting already described,[2] where thousands fell. Imagine a group of persons gathered together for worship and someone in the midst of the spirited singing or earnest exhortation suddenly uttering a piercing shriek and falling to the floor. Immediately others in all parts of the room would follow the example set, and many would lie prostrate. At a meeting held at Cabin Creek the latter part of May, 1801, the falling, crying out, praying, exhorting, singing, shouting, etc., were so general that few could escape without being affected. Those who tried to run were frequently struck on the way, or impelled by "some alarming signal" to return. The greatest number fell on the third night, and "to prevent their being trodden under foot . . . . they were collected together and laid out in order, on two squares of the meeting-house; which, like so many dead corpses, covered a considerable part of the floor."[3]

[1] A Presbyterian clergyman wrote, October, 1801, that he had attended three sacramental meetings at each of which between four and five thousand people attended. Everything was conducted with strict propriety. Those who fell were quietly taken care of and quiet reigned (Gallaher, *op. cit.*, 38–49).

[2] Chap. iii.   [3] McNemar, *The Kentucky Revival*, 23, 24.

In July of the same year a general (union) meeting was held at Indian Creek, Harrison County, Kentucky. Though prayer, exhortation, singing, shouting, and leaping for joy were generally indulged in, there was little of "that power which strikes conviction to the heart of the sinner" until about two o'clock in the afternoon of the third day.

"A boy from appearance about twelve years old retired from the stand in time of preaching under a very extraordinary impression and having mounted a log at some distance, and raising his voice, in a very affecting manner, he attracted the main body of the people in a few minutes. With tears streaming from his eyes he cried aloud to the wicked, warning them of their danger, denouncing their certain doom if they persisted in their sins, expressing his love to their souls and desire that they would turn to the Lord and be saved."

Supported by two men he spoke nearly an hour. When his strength seemed quite exhausted, he raised his hand and dropping his handkerchief wet with tears and perspiration, cried out: "Thus, O sinner! shall you drop into hell unless you forsake your sins and turn to the Lord. At that moment some fell like those who are shot in battle, and the work spread in a manner that human language cannot describe."[1] A girl about ten years old was struck at another meeting, and when able to

[1] McNemar, *op. cit.*, 25, 26.

speak began to exhort, continuing two hours in prayer and exhorting. At Point Pleasant, Kentucky, a man over fifty, disbelieving in the exercises, brought a staff with a sharp nail in the lower end for the purpose of prodding those who fell and making them start up. While warmly disputing with one of those in favor of the exercises, he fell down and remained speechless for about an hour. When he recovered he confessed the trick he had intended playing, and acknowledged his sins. One young woman on the way to meeting wished if she fell down it might be into hell. She caught the exercise and remained in a torpor "which has lasted three weeks."[1] An intelligent deist in the neighborhood of Cain Ridge at the beginning of the revival said to Mr. Stone, "I always thought before you were an honest man; but now I am convinced you are deceiving the people." Mr. Stone, reported, "I viewed him with pity and mildly spoke a few words to him. Immediately he fell as a dead man, and rose no more until he confessed the Savior."[2] It was not unusual for people who had gone to meetings to ridicule the work to catch the contagion and fall like the others. A lady and gentleman of some note in the fashionable world were attracted to the

[1] *Draper MSS*, "Patterson Papers," No. 105, 3 MM (see Appendix VII for this letter).

[2] *Biography of Elder Barton W. Stone* (ed. 1853), 36, 37.

meeting at Cain Ridge. On the way they sportively agreed that if either of them should fall the other should remain and render suitable protection and assistance. They had been on the ground only a short time when the lady fell suddenly. Her companion fled at full speed; but had only gone a short distance when he too fell and was surrounded by a crowd.[1] The contagious nature of the exercise was soon recognized and many preachers warned their congregations not to attend. These warnings, however, simply served to increase the crowds, as each considered himself impervious. Dr. Thomas Cleland of Kentucky, a Presbyterian clergyman, relates that as a young man he went to the Cain Ridge meeting fully expecting to fall. To his disappointment the scene did not move him the first day. The day following, one of the preachers in his sermon described his condition so well that his eyes became "a fountain of tears." "I stood behind one of the benches leaning forward against its back. I wept until my handkerchief was saturated with my tears. I felt like giving way. I felt an indescribable sensation as when one strikes his elbow against a hard substance. . . . . My position was discovered by a friend near me." Several hours elapsed before he recovered.[2]

[1] Davidson, *History of the Presbyterian Church in Kentucky*, 149.

[2] Gillett, *History of the Presbyterian Church*, II, 168, n. 1.

The following formal letter written by a gentleman in Kentucky to his brother describes his own sensations at one of the large meetings:

The people known by the appellation of Presbyterians assembled on Friday last at Concord-meeting-house, by way of preparation for the Lord's Supper. I did not attend until the Sabbath, when I saw the ordinance administered and many people prostrate on the ground crying for mercy. I passed through the day as an impartial spectator, but frequently wrapt in amazement, involved in doubt, and anxious for certainty. . . . . I did not intend to return the following day. [Tormented by fears, however, he and his wife returned the following day to the meeting.] A more tremendous sight never struck the eyes of mortal man. The very clouds seemed to separate and give way to the praises of the people of God ascending to the heavens; while thousands of tongues with the sound of hallelujah seemed to roll through infinite space; while hundreds of people lay prostrate on the ground crying for mercy. Oh! my dear brother, had you been there to have seen the convulsed limbs, the apparently lifeless bodies, to all of which the distorted features exactly comporting, you would have been constrained to cry out as I was obliged to do, the gods are among the people; nor was this confined to the commonality alone; but people of every description lay prostrate on the ground. There you might see the learned Pastor, the steady patriot and the obedient son crying holy, holy, holy, Lord God Almighty: behold the honourable matron and virtuous maiden crying with all the appearance of heart-felt distress, Jesus thou son of the most high God, have mercy upon us. Cast your eyes a few paces farther, and there you might see the prodigal in the arms of the professed libertine, crying hosannah to God in the highest, there is no other name under heaven whereby the man can be saved, but by the name of Jesus. See the poor oppressed African with his soul liberated longing to be with his God.[1]

Some of those who fell had no previous warning, while others were seized by a peculiar tremor the moment before they fell. Many uttered piercing shrieks. A prickly sensation as if the hand or foot were asleep sometimes preceded the fall. An eyewitness thus describe the state of those who fell:

Some have had symptoms before they fell. They have felt it in the great artery of the thighs and arms, but like a shock closed in immediately to the heart. The heart swells, liking to burst the body; occasions shortness and quickness of breath. They become motionless. The feet and hands become cold. . . . . Others felt no approaching symptoms; but fall as if shot dead and do not recollect anything until they begin to recover.[2]

Another account tells us:

It is impossible to give an account of all the various shades of difference in the appearance of those who are affected. The following may serve as a general outline of the work: when a person begins to be affected, he generally sinks down in the place where he stood, and is for a few minutes overwhelmed in tears; he then makes a weeping noise—some person near lays hold of him—he shrieks aloud—and discovers a desire to be on his back—in this he is indulged—and a friend sits down and supports the

[1] *New York Missionary Magazine* (1802), 126, 127.

[2] *Draper MSS*, "Patterson Papers," No. 105, 3 MM (see Appendix VII for this letter).

head of the person in his lap. Every tear now leaves his eye and he shouts aloud for about 20 minutes. Meanwhile the features of his face are calm and regular. His voice becomes more and more feeble for about 20 minutes more. By this time he is speechless and motionless, and lies quiet perhaps an hour. During this time his pulse is rather lower than the usual state,—the extremities are cold, the skin fresh and clear, the features of the face full, the eyes closed, but not so close as in sleep. Speech and motion return in the same gradual manner; the features become more full than before. Pleasure paints the countenance as peace comes to the soul, and when faith is obtained the person rises up, and with most heavenly countenance shouts—"Glory to God." This extasy abates in about a quarter of an hour and the person is generally led away by a friend to his tent. Calm, mild, sedate pleasure marks the countenance for several days; and those who have been often exercised in this pleasing manner, shew sweet mixture of love and joy which no tongue or pen can describe.[1]

Another eyewitness thus describes the falling:

The persons who are struck are generally first observed to pay close attention to the preaching; then to weep and shed tears plentifully for a while; after this a twitching or yerking seizes them, and they fall to the ground helpless, and convulsed through their whole frame as if in the agonies of death. In the beginning of this awakening, it was common for those who fell after they had been lying for a while to speak in an astonishing manner as to length of time, matter, and loudness of voice. Some of the most powerful sermons I have heard from mortals came from

[1] *New York Missionary Magazine* (1802) 183 (letter from a Presbyterian minister, dated Waxhaw, Lancaster District, South Carolina, April 3, 1802).

the mouths of persons of the above description, unable to help themselves. Some have spoken almost without cessation for the space of five hours, and some parts of the time so loud that they might be heard at a distance of a mile. It appeared as difficult for them to refrain from speaking as it would be for a person under deep bodily distress to refrain from groaning. When entreated both by ministers and people to withhold they would say they could not. Some of them would try; but, in a minute or two, it would burst forth from them like a torrent. The cry has often been so great for a while that there was no such thing as ministers being heard in preaching or exhorting. When this was the case they would stop a while till the torrent of the cry should be over. Their great cry was their guilt and danger—their hard heart—their sin and criminality—that they should die—that they should be damned forever—that God would be infinitely just in sending them directly to hell. They would frequently cry, I deserve hell, but how can I bear it! One little boy in my congregation, one night, was crying bitterly. "O!" said he, "I am lost forever. I am going right down to hell. O, I see hell, and the breath of the Lord like a stream of brimstone kindling it."[1]

The one who fell would lie helpless for from fifteen minutes to twenty-four hours and even longer, sometimes perfectly motionless, yet conscious of everything going on about him, and at the same time experiencing visions so graphic as to seem a reality. Others were convulsed and lay writhing and screaming. Some, while prostrate,

[1] *Massachusetts Missionary Magazine*, I, 198, 199 (letter from Rev. Thomas Moore, dated Ten Mile, Pennsylvania, March 9, 1803).

lamented their deplorable condition as lost sinners, or proclaimed that they had hope through Christ, and urged their friends to fly to Christ, praying and exhorting them on the topic. In nearly all cases the pulse was weak and low, though at times higher than usual. "The sinews were generally corded as in nervous complaints and after heat and relaxation; rarely cramped."[1] During the trance no pain was felt. Even those who struck obstacles as they fell, or pounced about on the floor sustained no injury. A case is reported in which hartshorn was being applied to a stout young man who lay flat on his back. Some of the ammonia ran into his nostrils, but he took no notice of it.[2]

On recovery, the subject of the exercise usually rose with beaming countenance and related the experiences that had come to him, exhorting those about him to give their attention to sacred things, and to accept Christ as their Savior. Others rose under deep dejection of spirit, declaring there was no hope for them. People were sometimes struck down five or six times before they obtained "any comfortable view," and, even then, comfort did not necessarily follow. As it was customary for all who had fallen to exhort their fellows, even the children were eagerly listened to. Falling down

[1] Davidson, *History of the Presbyterian Church in Kentucky*, 144; Lyle, *Diary*, 18.

[2] *Ibid.*, 145.

came to be a regular feature of the revival meetings, and it was customary to estimate the success of the meeting by the numbers who were affected in that manner.

Some time after the beginning of the Great Revival a new exercise appeared in eastern Tennessee which came to be familiarly known as "the jerks." At first it was confined to spasmodic jerking of the forearm at short intervals; but later it affected every muscle, nerve, and tendon in the body. McNemar's description as that of an eyewitness is interesting.

> Nothing in nature could better represent this strange and unaccountable operation than for one to goad another, alternately on every side, with a piece of red-hot iron. The exercise commonly began in the head which would fly backward and forward, and from side to side with a quick jolt which the person would naturally labor to suppress but in vain, and the more any one labored to stay himself and be sober the more he staggered and the more rapidly his twitches increased. He must necessarily go as he was stimulated, whether with a violent dash on the ground and bounce from place to place like a foot-ball, or hop round with head, limbs and trunk, twitching and jolting in every direction, as if they must inevitably fly asunder. . . . . By this strange operation the human frame was commonly so transformed and disfigured, as to lose every trace of its natural appearance. Some times the head would be twitched right and left to a half round with such velocity that not a feature could be discovered, but the face appear as much behind as before, and in the quick progressive jerk, it would seem as if the person was transmuted into

some other species of creature. Head dresses were of little account among the female jerkers. Even handkerchiefs bound tight round the head would be flirted off almost with the first twitch, and the hair put into the utmost confusion, this was a very great inconvenience to redress which the generality were shorn, though directly contrary to their confession of faith. Such as were seized with the jerks wrested at once, not only from under their own government, but that of every one else so that it was dangerous to attempt confining them, or touching them in any manner, to whatever danger they were exposed.[1]

The "jerks" proved to be most contagious and the mere suggestion of them was sufficient to animate an entire congregation with this peculiar exercise. A Presbyterian clergyman, hearing that a neighboring congregation was afflicted with the exercise, went to remonstrate with them. He was seized himself while addressing them, and upon returning home communicated the malady to his own people which had assembled to hear the report of his visit. Another clergyman of the same denomination, a graduate of Princeton who had settled in Tennessee, would be seized in the pulpit, shout and hallo, jump down and run to the woods. After an interval he would return as calm and rational as ever. Peter Cartwright in his autobiography tells of a crowd of drunken rowdies that

[1] McNemar, *The Kentucky Revival*, 61, 62. McNemar adds, "yet few were hurt except it were such as rebelled against the operation, through wilful and deliberate enmity and refused to comply with the injunctions which it came to enforce."

came to break up a religious service. The leader, a stout man, cursed the jerks and all religion and, as so often happened, fell himself a victim. He tried to run, but jerked so powerfully that he could not get away. Finally he expired after a particularly violent jerk which broke his neck. As with the falling exercise, any time and place were favorable to the jerks and many avoided serious thoughts and refused to attend meetings, so easily was an attack brought on.

Peter Cartwright records that he had seen more than five hundred jerking at one time. Some would run; but could not get away. Those who resisted were the more severely exercised.

> To see those proud young gentlemen and young ladies dressed in their silks, jewelry, and prunella, from top to toe take the *jerks* would often excite my risibilities. The first jerk or so you would see their fine bonnets, caps and combs fly and so sudden would be the jerking of the head that their long loose hair would crack almost as loud as a waggoner's whip.[1]

On one occasion just after the sermon, a lively tune was suddenly started by someone in the audience. A young woman began to whirl around like a top. She continued for an hour without stopping, whirling at the rate of fifty times in a minute, complaining of pain or distress when the singing stopped. She had been subject to the jerks several

[1] *Autobiography of Peter Cartwright*, 20.

years.[1] Another eyewitness relates that ladies were seized with the jerks at the breakfast table as they were pouring tea or coffee. Sometimes the exercise was so severe that life was endangered.[2] Closely connected with the jerks was an exercise called barking. Short gutteral sounds similar to the barking of a dog often proceeded from those afflicted with jerking. A minister in lower Kentucky stated that

> it was common to hear people barking like a flock of spaniels on their way to meeting. . . . . There they would start up suddenly in a fit of barking, rush out, roam around, and in a short time come barking and foaming back. Down on all fours they sometime went, growling, snapping their teeth, and barking just like dogs.[3]

Voluntary dancing, another form of exercise, was encouraged as a means of warding off other disagreeable exercises.[4] It appeared some years after the revival began among certain Presbyterians in Kentucky and Ohio who were called New Lights because they "taught that the will of God was made manifest to each individual who honestly sought after it by an inward light, which shone into the heart."[5] Dignified clergymen sometimes set

---

[1] *Biblical Repertory*, VI (old series), 346.

[2] Young, *Autobiography of a Pioneer*, 136.

[3] Benedict, *A History of the Baptist Denomination in America* II, 256.

[4] McNemar, *The Kentucky Revival*, 62, 63.   [5] *Ibid.*, 29.

the example as in the case of John Thompson related by McNemar:

> At the spring sacrament at Turtle Creek in 1804 br. Thompson had been constrained just at the close of the meeting to go to dancing and for an hour or more to dance in a regular manner round the stand, all the while repeating in a low tone of voice—"This is the Holy Ghost—Glory!"[1]

Rev. Mr. Lyle, reported that he saw several young women leaping most nimbly at Point Pleasant in 1803. A young girl sprang a dozen times nearly two feet from the ground notwithstanding she was held by the hands.[2] In the winter of 1804 the Schismatics, as those in Kentucky and Ohio who had severed connection with the Presbyterian church were called, began to praise God in the dance, encouraging each other to unite in the exercise. Many justified themselves by scriptural quotations. The dancing is described as a gentle, not ungraceful, movement, with little variety in the step to the accompaniment of a lively tune. Some of those subject to visions declared that as they entered upon the heavenly scenes their whole soul and body were perfumed with a peculiar fragrance, which rendered everything mortal disagreeable and unsavory. Under the influence of this singular perfume, which seemed to answer to the scripture notion of the

[1] McNemar, *The Kentucky Revival*, 60.

[2] Davidson, *History of the Presbyterian Church in Kentucky*, 151, 152; Lyle, *Diary*, 106, 112.

smell of Christ's garments from the ivory palaces and all the powders of the merchant, "they would swoon away three or four times in a day, recover, rise and dance round with incarnate and elevated springs."[1] Other exercises appeared in many congregations. Sometimes the one affected would roll over and over like a wheel, regardless of a chance mud puddle or other obstacles that might happen to be in the way. Others would run with amazing swiftness, leaping over obstructions in the path. One young woman at Salem in 1802, having fallen, lay a great while, then, jumping up, cried as if distracted that others hindered her from serving God. For some time she pranced over the benches, then fell and lay as in a syncope.[2] One writer describes a peculiar singing exercise in which the subject in a very happy state of mind would sing most melodiously, not from the nose, or mouth, but entirely in the breast, the sounds issuing thence. This was the accompaniment of visions of the Holy City when those under its influence attempted to join in the songs of the angelic host.[3] A variety of other emotions designated by no particular name appeared in different localities, but did not become epidemic.

[1] McNemar, *op. cit.*, 66, 67.

[2] Davidson, *History of the Presbyterian Church in Kentucky*, 150, 151; Lyle, *Diary*, 59.

[3] McNemar, *op. cit.*, 66.

Trances and visions became common among those affected by the exercises. These in a measure fostered the prophetic spirit, and many declared that the millennium was at hand. This led to a singular mode of praying. "According to their proper name of distinction, they stood *separate* and *divided*, each one for one; and in this capacity, they offered up each their separate cries to God in one united harmony of sound, by which the doubtful footsteps of those who were in search of the meeting might be directed some times to the distance of miles."[1] Heaven, hell, and topics suggested by them were the themes upon which those possessed of the prophetic spirit dwelt. Great mischief was wrought by these visionary people. They possessed little common-sense and wielded almost unbounded influence over certain superstitious minds. A fatality came to be attached to the most trifling details of daily life which were performed in obedience to the power which controlled the individual.

Phenomena of the kind just described were by no means peculiar to the subjects of the Great Revival of 1800. History furnishes similar instances in all ages and among all peoples, varying slightly, it may be, in form, yet practically the same. Heathen deities have been honored and evil spirits placated by the same frenzies. Demoni-

[1] McNemar, *op. cit.*, 69.

acal possession, the witchcraft delusion, and the excitement attendant upon Protestant revivals in the eighteenth and early nineteenth century are all analogous. As early as the eleventh century in Europe diabolical possession took the form of epidemics of raving, jumping, dancing, and convulsion. In these epidemics women and children especially were afflicted. The Crusades and the Black Death were followed by similar epidemics in various parts of Europe. Visions and prophesying were a regular accompaniment of these epidemics among all peoples. In the fourteenth century (1374) in the lower Rhine country the frenzy broke out in most violent form. The cures attempted only increased the disease; the afflicted danced for hours until they fell exhausted. "Some declared that they felt as if bathed in blood, some saw visions, some prophesied." These epidemics seem to have originated in the wild revels of St. John's days, an adaptation of heathen ceremonies and Christian form. About the same time in Italy an epidemic of dancing and jumping prevailed. It was supposed to originate in the bite of the tarantula for which the dancing was a cure. It has survived in the Italian *tarantella*.

Inmates of nunneries were especially subject to emotional epidemics. In the fifteenth century in Germany, one of the inmates of a nunnery was seized with a passion for biting her companions.

The mania spread until most, if not all, of her fellow-nuns followed her example. The epidemic passed to other convents in Germany, Holland, and across the Alps into Italy. In a French convent, one of the nuns began to mew like a cat, and severe measures were required to check the contagion which soon affected the other nuns.

Two marked epidemics of similar character occurred in France early in the eighteenth century: one at the tomb of François de Paris, a Jansenist deacon buried in St. Medard cemetery, the other among the Huguenots in the mountains of Cévennes.[1] Such a pitch did the excitement reach in St. Medard, upon the report of miracles worked at the tomb, that the authorities were finally obliged to wall up the place; and even that did not stop the excitement which continued for some time, stimulated by earth brought from the tomb. The Huguenots who had fled to the Cévennes, under the continued persecution of Louis XIV reached an ecstatic state. Some of the peasants were seized with convulsions and began to prophesy. An epidemic followed. Men, and children especially, caught the contagion, comparatively few women being affected. Those affected fell to the

---

[1] For above and other examples see White, "Diabolism and Hysteria," *Popular Science Monthly*, XXXV, Robins, "Maenadism in Religion," *Atlantic Monthly*, LII, and Stoll, *Suggestion und Hypnotismus in der Völkerpsychologie* 347, 348.

Phenomena of the Revival

ground and were convulsively exercised, then rose to exhort those about them. So common did trembling become that they were called the "tremblers of Cévennes."

In Roman Catholic countries these seizures occurred often in convents, in churches where young girls were brought for first communion, and at "miracle shrines." In Protestant countries they accompanied great religious excitement. Here they were attributed, not as among the Catholics to Satan, but to the spirit of the Almighty.

England, Scotland, and Ireland in the eighteenth century furnish examples of emotional epidemics in revival seasons. John Wesley records numerous instances of persons falling to the ground under preaching "as if struck by lightning." In Cambuslang parish, Lanarkshire, Scotland, in 1742, numbers were convicted of sin under the preaching of the minister, an admirer of Whitefield, and were thrown into the greatest agony about the state of their souls. Not only did they utter most piercing cries, but their bodies were violently agitated; they clapped their hands, beat their breasts, shook, trembled, fainted, were convulsed, and sometimes bled copiously at the nose.[1] Again, in about 1774, swoons and convulsions similar to those in Kentucky became common in the parish of

[1] For examples in other countries see Davidson, *History of the Presbyterian Church in Kentucky*, 177–82.

Northmaven among the Shetland Islands. Fifty or sixty would sometimes be carried struggling or roaring into the yard, and they would rise perfectly unconscious of what had happened. The Jumpers, a Methodist sect which originated in Cornwall, still has its adherents in Wales, and presents the closest similarity to the jerker of the revival of 1800.

Those of the immigrants to America who had witnessed and participated in the revivals in the British Isles, recognized the exercises which made their appearance in the western country at the end of the eighteenth century as something with which they were already familiar.

In Colonial days under the preaching of Whitefield, Edwards, and the Tennents, similar excitement had prevailed in America, in a less marked degree. Reports from the James River region, in 1783, speak of an extraordinary revival in which it was not unusual to have a large proportion of the congregation prostrated, some motionless, others convulsively screaming, shouting, and bounding about on the floor. A Baptist preacher who traveled over the Blue Ridge about that time, in a region under revival, relates that it was not uncommon to hear the people, when religiously exercised, bark like dogs. In Kentucky, in 1790 and 1792 there were meetings attended by the falling and confusion which characterized the later movement.[1] In the revival of 1800 the striking feature was therefore not the exercises themselves, but the number of people who were affected by them. It is impossible to estimate the exact number who caught the contagion, but some idea can be gained when the size of the camp-meetings and the large area over which the revival spread are considered. It was no uncommon occurrence for several hundred to be affected at one time.

Great excitement followed the appearance of the convulsive exercises in the western part of the United States. Naturally a difference of opinion prevailed regarding them. Some from the first doubted their efficacy. Many looked upon them as the direct manifestation of the power of God. They believed and taught that the Spirit of God entered into the person so affected, and that therefore it was sinful to resist when impelled by the Spirit to cry out, or to fall, etc. Superstition was rife among the settlers in the wilderness, and the impression that the work was supernatural was firmly lodged in the minds of many. The leaders of the movement did all in their power to deepen

[1] Asbury, *Journal*, II. Garret, *Recollections of the West*, 15, thus describes Bishop Asbury's first visit to Kentucky: Crowds gathered day and night and "often the floor was covered with the slain of the Lord and the house and woods resounded with the shouts of the converted." (This account, written long after the events described, seems to blend together the meetings in 1790 and 1792.)

the impression. Scripture was cited to justify falling down, trembling, and dancing, and in every way the people were encouraged in the exercises. The result was confusion indescribable in the meetings. Often the preacher was silenced by the babel of voices about him. Little respect was paid to authority. But this utter disregard of conventionality soon aroused bitter opposition. The Presbyterians, especially, questioned the propriety of such worship. Great difference of opinion prevailed among the clergy of that denomination upon the subject of the revival. Churches were divided. The revival party, in several places in the region where the revival began, was denied entrance to the meeting-house and forced to worship elsewhere.[1] For various reasons those opposed to the form which the revival movement had taken did not at first make a determined stand. Some feared that they might check the movement altogether and were unwilling to do that. Others were puzzled, not knowing just how to regard the exercises, as many directly opposed to the extravagances often caught the infection and themselves became subjects of one or another form of exercise. The meetings, however, at length became so disorderly that the opposition was forced to take a decided stand. The preachers opposed to the excitement

[1] McDonnold, *History of the Cumberland Presbyterian Church*, 39, 40.

did all in their power to check the extravagances, and in their own congregations discouraged every effort to stir up the emotions. The enthusiastic revival leaders accused them of being deists. The conservative Presbyterians generally, and especially the members of the Associate Reformed church, were opposed to the work. These thought it enthusiasm, hypocrisy, possession of the devil, witchcraft, etc. Many attributed it to sympathy.

The revival movement met with encouragement among the Methodists, as it was in accord with their method of working. As to the value of the bodily exercises, however, there was a difference of opinion. The wiser leaders held them merely as means to an end, a few as an end in themselves. Bishop Asbury, when questioned as to his opinion of their value, replied that any persons who could not give an account of the convincing and converting power of God might be mistaken; falling down would not do.[1]

Among the Baptists, opposition to the extravagances seems to have prevailed generally. Benedict states that in the upper counties of Kentucky, where the revival was greatest among the Baptists, and in western Tennessee, they were not at all troubled by the bodily exercises, though these

[1] Asbury, *Journal*, III, 113.

prevailed considerably among them in the Green River region and eastern Tennessee.[1]

The revival extravagances were discredited by the better informed among the settlers generally. A large proportion of this class, not belonging to any one of the denominations represented in the West, were known as deists. The flexible term deist was made to include all who denied dogmatic Christianity. They are frequently mentioned in accounts of the revival. Though the deists themselves were not always superior to the bodily exercises, and often fell victims while looking on at the meetings, it may be inferred that they ridiculed the movement generally.

The value of the bodily exercises was greatly overrated. To many they took the place of vital religion, as they were supposed to work a decided change in the one subject to them. Too great stress was laid upon emotional piety. Little minds were overbalanced. Pride, censoriousness, and conceit were engendered in many. At one of the meetings a woman after writhing for some time "broke out into a kind of prayer in which she charged the ministers with coldness and deadness in religion, with too great attachment to the beggarly elements of this world, and with keeping back and discouraging the people of God. She

[1] Benedict, *A General History of the Baptist Denomination in America*, II, 256.

also avowed her belief that the absence of some of them that evening was owing to slothfulness and fondness of earthly objects."[1] Children were brought too prominently forward. The eager attention given to their exhortations by older and sometimes by educated people could but give them exalted opinions of themselves. The more imaginative, both young and old, were tempted to fabricate experiences in accord with the expectations of friends and neighbors. Chance, too, was given the unscrupulous to vent personal malice and to trade upon their susceptible neighbors. Many held that those subject to the exercises had uncommon attainment in evangelical piety and knowledge. This bred contempt for those whose opinions might happen to differ from the one expressed. Self-control was almost an unknown quantity in the revival meetings. Those who shouted the loudest, exhorted and prayed the longest, even though this might be to the point of utter exhaustion, were considered most blessed. Disrespect for the outward form of religion was general. The young convert in lofty tone would warn sinners to fly from the wrath to come, regardless of the fact that he might be drawing the attention from the minister's sermon. In fact, services were often taken in hand by converts who considered the pulpit of little

[1] Davidson, *History of the Presbyterian Church in Kentucky*, 169; Lyle, *Diary*, 102.

account, especially if inclined to formal sermonizing. Some would sleep through the sermon, rising to voice their own opinions the moment it was over.

Some were undoubtedly brought to consider religious matters by means of the exercises and were often transformed as a result. Yet on the whole the bodily exercises tended to bring religion into disrepute, and were merely condoned, when not actually discouraged, by the better educated in all denominations. The more candid and liberal-minded ascribed the exercises to the imperfections of agitated human nature, to the influence of strong passions, and to the force of sympathy and example aided by peculiar circumstances.[1]

Modern psychological inquiry has thrown a flood of light upon the revival of 1800 and all similar movements. The nervous system, with its network of cells and fibers, reacting upon impressions from the objective and subjective world, must be carefully considered in determining the causes underlying such periods of excitement. At the outset the emotions and the will demand attention. Emotion depends upon two factors, the organic element, that is, the nervous structure itself, and the external stimulus. In each case, therefore, the reaction upon a certain stimulus will be determined by the mentality of the particular individual

[1] Ramsay, *History of South Carolina*, II, 35, note.

receiving the stimulus. In many cases, mere suggestion is sufficient to provoke immediate reaction. The will plays a most important part in determining whether or not a certain definite stimulus shall be reacted upon, or the impulse to act inhibited. Yet even the will is, at times, in certain cases, powerless to prevent reaction, and muscular movement follows in spite of and in direct opposition to the will of the individual. The interfibral connection of the cells of the nervous system is so complex and intricate that the overcharging of one cell may lead to the discharging of cells other than the one directly stimulated, resulting in most unexpected reaction.

In considering phenomena such as the revival of 1800 presented in the bodily exercises, not only the mental state of those subject to the exercises, but the atmosphere surrounding them must be borne in mind. The individual by himself and the individual as an element in a large unit, as for instance the crowd, may present two very different mental aspects. Again and again, the revival reports make mention of the deist, the scoffer, or the merely curious onlooker who was seized by the particular exercise in vogue at the meeting he chanced to attend. Drawn in spite of himself into the spirit of the hour, he reacted upon the suggestion made by the vehement preacher, the animated song, or the loud-voiced exhortation of someone who had just recovered from an attack, and fell a prey to the exercise. At a meeting in North Carolina,

> several young men were struck down . . . . who came there as opposers, making boasts of what they would do if any were struck down in their presence, and defying all the ministers to strike them down. . . . . They appeared to be in the most agitated misery which it is impossible to conceive, or express, rolling and tumbling about for many hours in the greatest agitation, sometimes crying for mercy acknowledging the most accumulated load of guilt; then despairing to obtain mercy; then pleading again; praying for the souls of their little brothers and sisters . . . . for all the world of mankind and with the greatest apparent fervency and sincerity, that none of them might be called from time, before their peace was made with the Redeemer.[1]

Two men attended a sacramental meeting to investigate the excitement. They separated in the congregation and met again after the service. One of them said he thought it must be the work of God; the other hastily replied, "I am persuaded it is the work of the devil." Scarcely had he spoken, when his whole system seemed unnerved, and he tumbled headlong off a log upon which he had been standing.[2] A man, bitterly exasperated with his wife for remaining at the meeting-house all night, came and ordered her home, but she

[1] *New York Missionary Magazine* (1802), 312 (extract of letter dated Pendleton District, South Carolina, July 30, 1802, describing a camp-meeting).

[2] *New York Missionary Magazine* (1803), 334.

refused to go. He went home in anger. There he was struck with conviction and lay powerless on his own floor. Another left a sacrament, despising, and condemning all he saw as delusion and madness. The day following he fell down in the field while at work, and lay there until found by his family some time during the night.[1]

There is no doubt that the exercises were in many cases involuntary, as with the young woman, who, unconscious of any change, was amazed to find people flocking around her, until making an effort to move she found herself powerless to do so; and the man who fell while threatening to beat his swooning daughters if they ever came to such a place again. Others, again, so earnestly desired the exercises that they yielded to the first impulse which might have been controlled. Still others entered upon them voluntarily, impelled by the desire to attract attention and by various other motives. The morbid imitative faculty so strong in humanity had much to do with the epidemics which resulted from the efforts of various individuals to promote a revival at the end of the eighteenth century.

It is . . . . a law that the perception of the effects of emotion and proximity to those who are under the power thereof will produce upon many effects similar to those

[1] "McGready's Narrative of the Revival in Logan County," *New York Missionary Magazine* (1803), 236.

manifested before them, so that they will weep when others weep even though in no way related to the cause of grief. . . . . It is not . . . . so generally known that any special form of manifestation may become epidemic if believed to have a divine, or even a naturally necessary origin, and be indefinitely repeated.[1]

Hypnotic suggestion, too, induced many to take part. Those who attended the Great Revival meetings expected to experience certain feelings and to see certain results. This led to expectant attention with the usual result which follows the possession of the mind by a dominant idea.[2]

The style of preaching in vogue among the promoters of the revival stirred up the emotions to such a pitch that in many cases the very intensity of the emotion demanded some outward expression. The terrors of hell were so vividly portrayed that even the unimaginative were profoundly moved, and the more sensitive were so wrought upon that they actually felt in nascent form the evil pictured. Fear for themselves, for their relatives, their friends, their neighbors, so powerfully affected their imagination that they lost all self-control upon the slightest provocation, and either vented their feel-

[1] Buckley, *History of Methodism*, I, 262, 263.

[2] The continued concentration of the mind upon a certain idea gives the latter a dominant power, not only over the mind, but over the body. The muscles become involuntarily instruments whereby it is carried into operation, and the volitional power is for a time in abeyance (see Carpenter, *Mental Physiology*, 293).

Phenomena of the Revival 119

ings in unusual muscular activity, or fell motionless to the ground. Hope, engendered by the prospect of salvation and everlasting happiness, on the other hand affected other nervous centers and threw some into transports of joy, likewise expressed in various ways.

Women and children most readily responded to the emotional impulse. The excitement which became epidemic at the large meetings and in the smaller congregations was usually started by loss of self-control on the part of a child or a woman. Men, however, often fell victims to the epidemic which ensued, and at one of the smaller camp-meetings at Cain Ridge it is reported that those who fell were nearly all men.

Children react almost immediately to suggestion. A morbid tendency to self-examination was induced by the disheartening doctrinal preaching of impassioned men. This unduly affected the imagination of the young and awakened in them earnest solicitation in regard to the way of salvation. One of the Presbyterian ministers describing the revival in Kentucky in a letter to a friend wrote that prayer-meetings might be attended every day or night by riding a few miles; that boys of twelve or fifteen cheerfully took part in these societies when called on. It was not an uncommon sight on Sabbath evenings and frequently during the week to find twenty or more children, all under thirteen years of age, engaged in most solemn prayer; some crying to Jesus for mercy, some shouting "Glory to God for salvation," and praying for their own souls and the souls of others. This is not a hasty flash, but continues, and they become more dutiful and docile. "Their desire, as soon as they take the bodily exercise, for instruction and the means of grace is past conception."[1] This desire for instruction led often to protracted meetings and the loss of interest in everything save the one topic. The mind became overbalanced and an unlooked-for discharge of emotion could but follow.

The women, whose lives were more circumscribed than those of the men in many instances were easily moved by the suggestion of the hour. It was the women of the family who conversed most often with the itinerant preacher and were made to feel the awful responsibility of life. The religious instruction of the children fell to the mother generally. She was assisted, it is true, by the formal family worship conducted by the father; but the main responsibility rested with her. Thus women thought oftener of spiritual matters and were more keenly alive to suggestions along those lines.

The very atmosphere of life in the wilderness, the loneliness, the consciousness of danger, seen

[1] Gallaher, *The Western Sketch Book*, 53–57.

or unseen, the awful sense of human weakness in the presence of the mighty power that seemed to brood over the forest, rendered the mind susceptible to impressions, especially when ideas were presented with enthusiasm that riveted the attention. An innate craving for excitement drew the people to the place that promised variety after the monotonous round of daily duty. To a certain element of society the meeting-house, east of the mountains, had been the center of social life, and its absence in the sparsely settled regions was keenly felt. They craved public worship and the attendant social intercourse. This accounts in great measure for the instantaneous favor that greeted the camp-meeting. The unnatural excitement which resulted from days and nights spent in the abnormal atmosphere of the great meetings (characterized as they were by the absence of all regularity and the lack of proper nourishment and rest) wrought most powerfully upon the minds of those who might have resisted the impulse to react had they not been exhausted physically, as well as upon the minds of those naturally quick to respond to outward impressions. It was unusual for the more refined and cultured to be affected by the exercises, as is evinced by the reports which make special mention of the falling of "genteel persons." The better-educated class probably did not attend camp-meetings to any great extent. Methodist enthusiasm appeared crude to them, and they looked with disfavor upon emotional worship. In their eyes there was a fanaticism in a teaching which stripped life of even its milder pleasures and that absolutely forbade anything but the plainest apparel devoid of all ornaments.

Another feature of the revival which amazed those who witnessed it, and which modern psychological investigation can easily explain, was the surprising ease with which those who had undergone or were undergoing some form of exercise conversed and exhorted upon biblical themes. There was at that time no knowledge of the subliminal region of consciousness, that vast repository of impressions unconsciously received day by day. They were amazed to hear children of six and seven use language beyond their years, and could not know that this was the result of the Bible training so carefully provided for at home and in school.[1]

The cells which had stored up the impressions so received were discharged by the unwonted excitement which had affected the nervous system. It is an interesting fact that all affected by the exercises and those subject to trances and visions expressed themselves only in terms perfectly familiar to one acquainted with religious phrase-

[1] The children affected were usually from religious families, whose spiritual training had been a subject of anxious concern to their parents.

ology. The ideas were all suggested by, or taken directly from, the hymns, the Bible, and other books of a religious nature. Religious topics were frequently discussed by all classes of society. Hence it is not at all difficult to account for the "amazing language" of the scoffer or deist who caught the contagion.

In the medical world, the diseases of chorea, epilepsy, and hysteria are known to be attended with muscular movements and other symptoms identical with those displayed in the epidemics which attended the periods of great religious excitement already passed under review. Pathologically it is difficult to define exactly the epidemics which prevailed during the revival of 1800. A large number of cases fall under the head of chorea, hysteria, or ecstasy. Just what proportion of the cases were epileptic cannot be ascertained. Undoubtedly there were epileptic seizures. Blood-letting and all remedial measures known at that time were resorted to to restore consciousness and quiet the convulsive movements; but these availed but little.

Such was the nervous excitement attendant upon the revival meetings that the inflection of the voice was sufficient to start the exercises. These did not usually occur, with any frequency, until meetings had been in progress some hours, or a day or two. Badly ventilated, overcrowded rooms must in a measure be held responsible for much of the excitement. It is interesting to note the experiments made by those who were opposed to such emotional displays. One Presbyterian clergyman, after a smooth and gentle course of expression, would suddenly change his voice and language to express something awful and alarming, and instantly a score or more would simultaneously be jerked forward from their seats, making a suppressed noise, similar to the barking of a dog. Thus the exercises would continue or abate according to the tenor of his discourse. This same man relates that a pious woman of his acquaintance was instantly set jerking by a change in the nature of their conversation. They were riding along, talking of ordinary matters, when he introduced a religious topic, and she immediately began to jerk forward and backward in her saddle. (She had previously been subject to the exercises.[1]) On one occasion, just as the preacher was about to give out the last hymn, an enthusiastic man in the crowded audience started a song with a lively tune. Several young women began to jerk backward and forward.[2] Jacob Young, one of the younger Methodist preachers, attended a camp-meeting at Carter's Station in eastern Tennessee in 1804. In his sermon he undertook to account for the jerks

[1] *The Biblical Repertory*, VI (old series), 343, 344.
[2] *Ibid.*, 345.

and spoke of the jerks as a judgment on that wicked community, enlarging on the intolerant spirit and religious bigotry which prevailed there. "I made a pause, and exclaimed at the top of my voice, 'Do you leave off jerking if you can.'" It was thought more than five hundred began jumping, shouting, and jerking. (There had been no previous appearance of the jerks in the meeting.[1])

Those opposed to the excitement soon realized that the attitude of the preacher had a great influence upon the character of the meeting. A peremptory command from him upon the first appearance of undue excitement sufficed in most cases to quiet those affected, and prevented contagion. A Baptist minister who was preaching where one of the jerkers began his motions made a pause, and in a loud and solemn tone said, "In the name of the Lord I command all unclean spirits to leave this place." The jerker immediately became still. David Benedict remarks that those who encouraged the exercises had enough of them to attend to.[2] Preaching upon such texts as: "Bodily exercise profiteth little," and "Let all things be done decently and in order" had a powerful effect in checking any tendency to disorder. Prayer proved the most effective remedy for those liable to jerking.

[1] *Autobiography of a Pioneer* (Rev. Jacob Young), 138, 139.

[2] Benedict, *A General History of the Baptist Denomination in America*, II, 256.

McGready tells the story of a young man, the son of an elder, who feigned illness one Sabbath because he did not wish to attend camp-meeting with his family. As he lay in bed, his mind ran upon the scenes being enacted at the camp-meeting, dwelling particularly upon a certain woman under exercise. Suddenly, to his astonishment, he was jerked out of the bed and all around the room. He never had been subject to the bodily exercises before and could not control himself. Remembering that he had heard of prayer as a remedy, he tried it and found it effective. He thought it all a dream, or illusion, and returned to bed. Again he thought of the meeting, the result was a violent repetition of the jerking. He arose and dressed, went out in the yard, and, to divert his mind, decided to work on a dogskin that needed unhairing. He drew it out of a vat, laid it upon the beam, rolled up his sleeves, and lifted the graining knife to begin. The knife was immediately flirted out of his hand and he was jerked backward and about the yard. Prayer again relieved him. He set to work again, with the same result. By this time he was thoroughly frightened, especially as even prayer failed to restore him readily. He ordered one of the slaves to put the work away and retired to his room, weeping and crying to God for mercy. There the family found him on its return.[1]

[1] *The Biblical Repertory*, VI (old series), 344, 345.

A physician in Illinois, about 1823, stated that he repeatedly witnessed the jerks in that part of the country, the persons subject to them being usually young women in the humbler walks of life who had moved to Illinois from states where the excitement had been great during the revival of 1800. When he wrote, the exercise was equally prevalent among the Methodists and Cumberland Presbyterians,[1] excited by passionate discourses addressed to fears and sympathies, and by animated singing.

From the sexes and age most susceptible, and the condition they occupy in society, the causes which excite and the effect produced, I conclude it a nervous disease brought on by continual mental excitement and protracted by habit. After it has become habitual from long continued mental excitement, sympathy suffices to call it into action.[2]

It is evident that no supernatural agency is necessary to explain the peculiar bodily exercises that attended the Great Revival in the western country. The individual, seized either at home or in public, had, previous to the seizure, received some suggestion through the sense of sight or hearing that resulted in bodily reaction.

The effect produced by these exercises and the general results of the Great Revival will be considered in the next chapter.

[1] Chap. v, see pp. 145, 146, on the origin of Cumberland Presbyterians.

[2] *The Biblical Repertory*, VI (old series), 351, 352.

CHAPTER V

THE RESULTS OF THE REVIVAL

A movement so far-reaching as the revival under consideration could not but exert a powerful influence upon the communities affected by it. In dealing with social problems, there is always room for wide difference of opinion as to the proportion of good and evil in any particular movement. Undoubtedly the extravagances which characterize the Great Revival in the West did much to degrade, in the minds of the more thoughtful, the very ideals so vehemently insisted upon by its earnest promoters. Granted also that the disorderly scenes, so much deplored by the most enlightened among all denominations, which made the camp-meeting attractive to the morally degraded, were detrimental to the highest interests of humanity. Making all due allowance for the excessive stress laid upon the emotional side of the religious life, yet it remains clear that the Great Revival stimulated the religious life of the country as a whole, and did much to develop the region west of the Alleghanies. A resident of Tennessee, in a letter dated Dixons Springs, Tennessee, May 13, 1843, wrote that he witnessed much of the excitement and, "notwithstanding all this fanaticism, much good appears to have been done."[1]

The results may perhaps best be considered from the standpoint of the individual, the community, and the denominations most vitally affected, with due consideration of the camp-meeting, the impetus given to missionary activity, and the propagation of the gospel, generally. In dealing with the effect of the revival upon the Presbyterian denomination, attention will be given to the schism which resulted in the formation of the Cumberland Presbyterian church. In this same connection, the

[1] "I know not whether you have ever heard of the great revival of religion which took place in this country in 1800 (and continued for several years), the most extraordinary in many respects that has been witnessed in modern times anywhere. It commenced with the Presbytereans, in Logan County, Ky., say 50 miles from here, and spread to a great extent, in every direction, and gave rise to Camp Meetings. Its first movement was under the ministry of James McGready, a zealous and talented Presbyterean preacher. The Methodists fell in and, with the others, joined in Communion, which has been kept up, though rather nominally, ever since. The Baptists stood aloof.

"It gave rise to a division among the Presbytereans. . . . . The exercises were various and most extraordinary, as jerks, dancing, running, jumping, wrestling, laughing, &c. Much of this, I witnessed myself, and not withstanding all this fanaticism, much good appears to have been done. This revival of religion with its concomitants, constitutes an important item in the history of the west." (This excerpt is taken from the postscript of a letter to L. C. Draper. This letter bears the autograph signature of William Martin, though it is not in his handwriting [*Draper MSS*, 3 XX, 18].)

history of the New Light movement, another defection from the Presbyterian body, and the foothold gained by the Shakers in northern Kentucky and Ohio will be considered.

Viewing the revival from the standpoint of the effect upon the individuals who came under its influence, it is impossible to determine, save in the most general way, what proportion of the thousands of men, women, and children who witnessed the excitement and were subjects of the bodily exercises were seriously affected; that is to say, were so affected that a change for the better was noticeable in their lives. Many professing Christians were deeply moved, and endeavored to live more in harmony with their profession. There is no doubt that many who joined the churches dated their conversion from one or another revival meeting. The various denominations reported greatly increased membership.

This increase among the Baptists in Kentucky alone when the revival was at its height serves to illustrate the remarkable gain. The Elkhorn Association[1] received by baptism 1,148 members in the year 1801. The Salem Association, in the course of three years, added more than 2,000 to its membership.[2] Comparing the Baptist churches

[1] Benedict, *A General History of the Baptist Denomination in America*, II, 242.

[2] *Ibid.*, II, 243.

of Kentucky and the number of communicants in 1800 and 1803, a gain of 113 churches and about 10,000 members is found by the latter date.[1] The Methodists in a single year added, in the bounds of the Western Conference, 3,250 members.[2] The year following, 3,000 more were added. The Presbyterians, among whom the movement originated, also reported most unusual accessions to their membership. The General Assembly minutes for 1803 record that several thousands had been brought to embrace the gospel of Christ in the Presbyterian church during the revival which was still in progress. Lee, in his history of the Methodists, states that the account in newspapers and private papers, by ministers and Christians generally, of the number of souls converted at campmeetings and other meetings far exceeded anything of the kind he had ever heard of before in the United States.[3] A large proportion of these converts were young people from pious families who

[1] Humphrey, *Revival Sketches*, 195: "A record of the Baptist churches in Kentucky states that 'in the remarkable outpouring of the Holy Spirit from 1799–1803 in most parts of our land, among different denominations, about ten thousand were added to the Baptist churches within that state who gave evidence of genuine conversion'"; cf. also Benedict, *op. cit.*, II, 251.

[2] Report of William McKendree, October 8, 1801, in John Atkinson, *Centennial History of American Methodism*, 483.

[3] Lee, *A Short History of the Methodists in the United States*, 283; letter from W. M. Kendree (probably William McKendree) dated October 10, 1802, in *Extracts of Letters*, 39–42; see Appendix VIII for this letter.

were by this means usually brought into the churches to which their parents belonged. The influence thus exerted in the majority of cases was probably lasting, to the extent, at least, of a nominal interest in spiritual concerns. "The Rev. Dr. Cleland wrote, in 1834, after witnessing the fruits of this work for more than thirty years. The work at first was no doubt a glorious work of God. 'Many within my knowledge became hopefully pious, the most of whom continue unto this present, and many have fallen asleep in Jesus. The number of apostates was much fewer than I supposed.'"[1] On the other hand, many of those who were carried away by the excitement of the hour gave no evidence of a change in their lives. The nervous seizure made no lasting impression. Still others, disgusted with the emotional extravagances which characterized the meetings, were led to ridicule all religion.

Turning to the effect upon the community, it is evident that the moral tone of many localities was raised. Rev. Manasseh Cutler, in a letter dated April 7, 1802, states that he had learned through a member of Congress from Kentucky[2] that the change, generally produced in the temper and manners of the people, wherever the revival

[1] Humphrey, *Revival Sketches*, 196.

[2] Thomas T. Davis (*Life, Journal and Correspondence of Rev. Manasseh Cutler*, II, 102).

had spread, was as pleasing and happy as it was astonishing. Rev. David Rice in a sermon at the opening of the synod of Kentucky in 1803 dwelt on the beneficent character of the revival in that section of the country. "A considerable number of persons appear to me to be greatly reformed in their morals. This is undoubtedly the case within the sphere of my particular acquaintance. Yea, some neighborhoods, noted for their vicious and profligate manners are now as much noted for their piety and good order. Drunkards, profane swearers, liars, quarrelsome persons, etc., are remarkably reformed."[1] An eyewitness wrote (the revival) "has confounded infidelity, awed vice into silence, and brought numbers beyond calculation under serious impression."[2] The minutes of the General Assembly of the Presbyterian church for the year 1803 record a change in the general aspect of society from dissoluteness and disorder to sobriety, order, and comparative purity. That there was much improvement still to be desired, especially in the life of the towns, is not to be denied. But the earnest spirit engendered by the revival was keenly alive to moral disorders and sought to improve the condition at large by eradicating vice and intemperance in the individual and stimulating

[1] Speer, *The Great Revival of 1800*, 61–64.

[2] Gallaher, *The Western Sketch Book*, 48 (letter from Rev. George Baxter to Rev. A. Alexander, January 1, 1802).

him to devote time and thought to the things that make for righteousness.

In considering the effect of the revival upon the denominational life of the West, it will be necessary to deal in detail with the three denominations most vitally affected by the excitement—the Presbyterians, Baptists, and Methodists. As already stated the membership in each of these denominations increased at an astonishing rate.[1] On the whole, however, the movement was detrimental to Presbyterian interests in the West, owing to the schisms which occurred in that society in Kentucky and Tennessee as the direct result of the revival movement. Great opposition to the bodily exercises had been manifested by many of the Presbyterian preachers, and they were not slow in making their objections known. The result was bitter controversy between the revivalists and the anti-revivalists in that church in eastern Kentucky. It was impossible to reconcile the differences between the two parties. The opposition strove to maintain the established forms of worship, and had no patience with the disorderly meetings of the revivalists. The teachings of the revivalists were subversive of ecclesiastical authority. They

[1] During the Great Revival, the four Baptist churches of South Elkhorn, Clear Creek, Bryan's Station, and Great Crossing received in one year 1,378 members (Benedict, *A General History of the Baptist Denomination in America*, II, 230).

claimed for each convert an inner light in the soul which interpreted the Scripture and directed the worship, regardless of accepted interpretation and prescribed forms. In the autumn of 1803, two members of the synod of Kentucky were charged with disseminating doctrines contrary to the Presbyterian Confession of Faith. The presbytery of Washington had put Richard McNemar, a revival preacher, on trial for preaching anti-Calvinistic doctrines. In September, 1803, his case was tried before the synod of Kentucky. Four other revival preachers united with McNemar knowing that their fate was bound up with his, and drew up a protest against the action of the synod, declaring their independence of that body and their withdrawal from its jurisdiction, claiming, however, still to be in communion with the church at large. The public reading of this document caused a sensation. A committee was appointed to confer with the five members, but all efforts at reconciliation proved futile. The synod then suspended the five members. Division and commotion resulted in the churches.[1] The suspended members at once constituted themselves into the presbytery of Springfield. McNemar wrote that they voluntarily withdrew from under

[1] *Autobiography of Barton W. Stone*, found in Rogers, *The Cane Ridge Meeting-House*, 165–69; B. B. Tyler, *History of the Disciples of Christ*, 24–26.

the jurisdiction of the Presbyterian church that they "might not be wholly left without the usual claim of congenial descent from Leo the Great."[1] These men did not intend to found a church or distinct party, but formed the new presbytery "to cover the truth from the impending storm and check the lawless career of opposition."[2]

These five seceding ministers, Richard McNemar, John Thompson, Robert Marshall, John Dunlevy, and Barton W. Stone, were popular with their congregations which largely seceded with them. These seceders were called by various names: New Lights, Schismatics, Stoneites, and Marshallites. For some months after separation, the Presbyterian mode of government was practiced. In April, 1804, the seceders decided to adopt the Scriptures as their only rule of faith and practice, the only standard of doctrine and discipline. The church as then constituted was to transact all business which concerned its members. The use of tokens was dispensed with, and the members were to call each other "brother and sister."

The peculiar worship of the churches thus constituted is interesting. They held that God and Christ had their abode in the soul of man, and that any exercise that accorded with the inward feelings of love and power and tended to their increase was

[1] McNemar, *The Kentucky Revival*, 42.
[2] *Ibid.*

acceptable to God as worship. It was customary to give the right hand of fellowship to those who entered their communion. Finding that this increased the inward working of the Spirit, it was gradually introduced as an act of worship, together with the singing of hymns and spiritual songs.

The whole society, old and young, male and female would commonly unite in this mode of worship, and taking each other by the hand would shake, not only their hands, but their whole bodies, like one churning, with such violence that the place would seem to quiver under them.

They called this rejoicing, "according to the observation of br. Stone, when he first heard the doctrine [new doctrine of atonement] stated, 'that if these things were established as truth he would rejoice forever.'" They encouraged the voluntary performance of the bodily exercises with public testimony of views and feelings attendant thereon. On this principle, voluntary dancing was introduced.[1]

The Schismatics conceived they were worshiping God to acceptance, while relating their conversion, expressing their abhorrence of sin, and singing spiritual songs to that effect—"I shall be holy here"—shaking hands and shuddering with indignation against their soul enemies —crying out for final deliverance from them.—"Make me Saviour, what thou art: live thyself within my heart."—Leaping and skipping voluntarily in the joyful hope—"Then the world shall always see Christ the holy child in me."

[1] See chap. iv, p. 87.

They endeavored to reclaim their fellows by a peculiar praying match. As it was contrary to their rules for one to attack another openly, they had recourse to the spirit, and by the brightest, boldest, and loudest gift of prayer, the cause was commonly decided. In this way they generally settled their controversies of every kind. One would begin to preach or exhort, and if his doctrine were judged unsound, or uninteresting, he would be presently matched with a prayer, and whichever collected the greatest warmth and manifested the most lively sensation of soul, gained the victory, and interested the general shout on that side.[1]

The exercises of jerking, barking, and rolling described in chap. iv played an important part in their worship. They made much of visions. Sleeping and waking, there was but one topic: the increasing work of God and the blessed Kingdom just about to appear.

These churches were all nominally under the presbytery of Springfield which had been constituted by the seceding party in 1803. In June, 1804, the dissolution of this body was announced in a curious pamphlet, entitled *The Last Will and Testament of the Presbytery of Springfield*. The preamble declared that body to be in "more than ordinary bodily health, growing in size and strength daily, and in perfect soundness and composure of mind." Knowing, however, that all delegated bodies must die once and "considering that the

[1] McNemar, *The Kentucky Revival*, 58–61.

life of every such body is very uncertain," the presbytery issued its will. The leaders desired that the body so dissolved might sink into union with the Body of Christ at large. Then followed statements of their idea of church government, the ordination and support of ministers, and the recommendation of the Bible as the only sure guide to heaven.[1] The members of the church began to call themselves Christians and their church the Christian church.[2] Their plan was to form a universal kingdom in which all denominations should unite. The fiery zeal of these people subjected them to persecution, as evinced in a letter written by Barton Stone, in 1805.

The floods of earth and hell are let loose against us, but me in particular. I am seriously threatened with imprisonment. . . . . Kentucky is turning upside down. The truth pervades in spite of man—Cumberland is sharing the same fate.[3]

[1] "Last Will and Testament of Springfield Presbytery," in McNemar, *The Kentucky Revival; Autobiography of Barton W. Stone* in Rogers, *The Cane Ridge Meeting-House,* 173–79.

[2] Stone, *Address to the Christian Churches in Kentucky, Tennessee, and Ohio* (1821), 97: "We have taken the name of Christians . . . . because we knew it was the name first given to the disciples of Jesus by divine authority. It better agreed with our spirit which is to unite with all Christians, without regard to names or distinctions." He then points out that there were too many party names already, that they had been called New Lights and Schismatics—the former a name given to many others, "indeed to every sect of living Christians in my remembrance for years past. . . . . We profess no new light."

[3] McNemar, *The Kentucky Revival,* 78.

The absolute freedom of worship guaranteed to each member of the Christian church, under the New Light principle, was a potent argument against continued unity. Of the five ministers who seceded in 1803, two joined the Shakers (McNemar and Dunlevy), two returned to the Presbyterian church (Marshall and Thompson), and one only (Barton W. Stone) remained true to the views then announced and finally in 1832 joined forces with the Christian church, organized by Alexander Campbell.[1]

This Christian church, or Church of the Disciples, also sought the union of all believers. It originated in western Pennsylvania, and was the outgrowth of the Christian Association of Washington, Pennsylvania. This association was organized about 1808, under the leadership of Thomas Campbell, a minister of the Associate Presbyterian church, who had come from Ireland in 1807. Thomas Campbell was much distressed at the discord and lack of unity in the church as a whole, and sought to harmonize existing differences. His gifted son, Alexander Campbell, who joined his father in 1808, was in sympathy with this spirit. Though regretting an addition of another to the already too numerous sects, they decided to con-

[1] Tyler, *History of the Disciples* (*American Church History*, Vol. XII), 72, 73; *Autobiography of Barton W. Stone* in Rogers, *The Cane Ridge Meeting-House*, 200, 201.

stitute the Association of Washington a church, in the year 1810. The aim of the new church was to follow as closely as possible the teaching of the Holy Spirit in the sacred writings. The New Testament was to be its constitution; its creed, belief in Jesus as the Son of God. Weekly communion was practiced from the first; and baptism by immersion was early deemed the only scriptural mode of baptism. Overtures were made to this society by the Baptists, and in 1813, the church became a member of the Redstone Association. Differences of opinion could not, however, be adjusted, and finally in 1827 the Mahoning Association, of which Alexander Campbell had become a member, adjourned *sine die* in the belief that there was no scriptural warrant for its existence. A few years later, many of the New Light churches joined the followers of Alexander Campbell. Shortly after, the Christian church, which has been an important factor in the religious life of the Middle West, was organized as a separate denomination. Its creed is substantially the same as that of the Washington Association of western Pennsylvania already referred to. Constant study of the Scriptures and the endeavor to apply them as the rule and practice of daily life were the foundation principles of this new denomination.

The New Light schism also prepared the ground for the development of Shakerism in the West.

This strange sect originated in England during the eighteenth century, its official title being "The United Society of Believers in Christ's Second Appearing.". The more familiar name of Shakers was given to its adherents because of the violent tremblings and shakings which seized them under the influence of strong religious emotion. The founder of the society, which traces its origin back to the French Prophets, was a woman, Ann Lee —"Mother Ann" as she was called by her followers. Divine revelations were received through her, the best known of which is the principle of celibacy. Just before the American Revolution, "Mother Ann" and several of her disciples migrated to New York and settled at Watervliet near Albany. Several years after the death of Ann Lee the society was organized on its present communistic basis. These communities are agricultural, and everyone performs his share of labor. They have today a reputation for thoroughness, frugality, and temperance. This has not, however, always been the case, as their peculiar mode of worship, devoid of external ordinances,[1] gave rise to all sorts of scandalous charges. This mode of worship, they claim, is due to the operation of the supernatural

[1] Dancing and marching to the accompaniment of song, shouting, and clapping of hands, with other emotional features.

power and light.[1] They believe that the second coming of Christ was accomplished in the life of Ann Lee, "the first mother, or spiritual parent, in the line of the female." The Kingdom of God had therefore been established, and the millennium was at hand.

Three men from the Shaker community in Canaan, New York, appeared in eastern Kentucky in 1805 and were welcomed by certain members of the New Light faction. Their teaching, that the Shaker doctrine was the culmination of the revival then in progress, appeared plausible to these revivalists, filled with the idea that a great change was to occur that very year, and they soon made converts. By the year 1806, a number of Shaker communities had been formed in Kentucky and Ohio. They met with bitter opposition from the New Lights who, in turn, subjected them to persecution. The usual result followed; their numbers were increased and Shakerism gained a strong foothold in Kentucky and Ohio especially, as a result of the Great Revival.

While the Presbyterian church was struggling with the New Light defection in eastern Kentucky, another schism threatened in the region that had given birth to the Great Revival. The difficulty here grew out of the impossibility of providing ordained ministers in sufficient numbers to meet

[1] They believe in constant intercourse with the spiritual world and claim at times to enjoy the various gifts of the apostles.

the increased demands for preaching. The difference of opinion between the friends and enemies of the Great Revival was as marked as in the eastern part of the state.

Most of the settlers had been accustomed to church privileges in their former homes and were clamorous for them in their frontier cabins. Those who attended the camp-meetings returned to spread the religious interest in their neighborhoods. A sufficient supply of preachers could not be secured. The case was one of extreme urgency. The Rev. David Rice visited McGready's field and being informed of the destitute state of most of the churches and the pressing demands for the means of grace, earnestly recommended that they should choose from among the laity some men who appeared to possess talents and a disposition to exercise their gift publicly to preach the gospel although they might not have acquired that degree of education required by the Book of Discipline. This proposition was cordially approved by both preachers and people. . . . . In almost every congregation that had been blessed with the outpouring of the Holy Spirit, there were one or more intelligent and spiritual men whose gifts in exhortation had already been honored by the Head of the Church in awakening and converting precious souls." Alexander Anderson, Finis Ewing, and Samuel King were encouraged by the revival preachers to prepare written discourses and to present themselves before the Transylvania Presbytery at its session in 1801. . . . . The proposition met with decided opposition in the meeting of the Presbytery, but after a protracted discussion it was agreed that they might be permitted to read their discourses privately to Mr. Rice. Mr. Rice reported favorably and they were then sent out as exhorters to the vacant congregations. So great was the demand for preachers that these men were all licensed to preach in the fall of 1802, in spite of the prejudice of the Presbyterian church in favor of pastors trained along certain well-defined lines.[1]

The proceedings which had resulted in the licensing of these men as preachers by the Transylvania presbytery caused great dissatisfaction in the synod of Kentucky. In the minds of those who opposed the step a more serious difficulty than the fact that these men lacked the regular training was the fact that, in subscribing to the Westminster Confession of Faith, they were allowed to make certain reservations which practically amounted to denial of leading tenets of the church. All efforts to adjust the difficulty proved futile. During the proceedings, the Cumberland presbytery, formed from the Transylvania presbytery in 1802, and made up almost entirely of those in favor of the revival movement, was dissolved. Finally in February, 1810, three of the revival preachers—Finis Ewing, Samuel King, and Samuel McAdow—constituted themselves an independent presbytery, called, after the one dissolved during the quarrel, the Cumberland presbytery.[2] This

[1] McDonnold, *History of the Cumberland Presbyterian Church* 48, 49 (quoting from James Smith, *History of the Christian Church*); Mss Minutes of Transylvania Presbytery.

[2] McDonnold, *History of the Cumberland Presbyterian Church*, chaps. vii–xi. In 1812 this Cumberland presbytery formed two others and the year following the first synod was organized, October, 1813, with sixteen ordained ministers within its bounds.

was the beginning of the Cumberland Presbyterian church which recognized the Confession and Discipline of the Presbyterian church as its standard, while at the same time it made provision for those who could not accept the doctrine of predestination as taught by that church. In form of worship the Cumberland Presbyterians resembled the Methodists rather than the body from which they seceded. Indeed, at one time, before the separation, some of the leaders wished as a body to unite with the Methodist church.[1] When the first synod was organized in October, 1813, the Cumberland Presbyterians had sixty congregations grouped under three presbyteries. From its inception this church gained steadily in numbers and influence and accomplished great good in those regions where it originated and farther west as settlements were established beyond the Mississippi.

Thus the Presbyterian church in Kentucky and western Tennessee especially lost many of its preachers and members. Some idea of the defection may be gained from the Assembly Reports of the condition of the church in 1803 and 1804. In the former year there were 31 presbyteries, 322 ministers, and 48 probationers, as compared with 27 presbyteries, 130 ministers, and 33 probationers in 1804.

[1] *Autobiography of Peter Cartwright*, 47, 48.

The prospect of the strengthening of the Presbyterian denomination, which the increased membership, in the years 1798-1803, promised, was blighted by the schism just reviewed. Presbyterian interests in the West were seriously affected, and the church did not easily regain its position of prominence in that region. Dr. Alexander, a Presbyterian minister, commented thus on the situation: "The truth is—and it should not be concealed—that the general result of this great excitement was an almost total desolation of the Presbyterian churches in Kentucky and part of Tennessee."[1]

Among the Baptists and Methodists, the general result of the Great Revival was to strengthen and build them up as denominations. Benedict maintains that this revival caused changes in the tone and efforts of the Baptists, and resulted in an enlargement of their boundaries. The wonderful accounts circulated by private letters, by the association minutes, and pamphlets "led the long-despairing and persecuted Baptists to thank God and take courage."[2] The differences between the Regular and Separate Baptists which had divided that society in the West were adjusted, and the two branches united early in the Great Revival.[3]

---

[1] Davidson, *History of the Presbyterian Church in Kentucky*, 189, note (letter dated September 5, 1846).

[2] Benedict, *Fifty Years among the Baptists*, 20, 21.

[3] Riley, *Southern Baptists*, 119.

The Methodist church in the West seems, on the whole, to have profited most by the Great Revival. By 1805 nearly 12,000 communicants were reported in the bounds of the Western Conference, a region in which the Methodists, five years earlier, had numbered only about 2,700 members.[1] The revival movement was more in line with their usual methods of working, and brought their doctrine and discipline forward most prominently. The result was an increased respect for the denomination, which constituted it a most important factor in the development of the western country.[2] There was an adaptability about the Methodist system that rendered it peculiarly fitted to the needs of a pioneer community. No other denomination understood so well the needs of the immigrant. The circuit rider with his tireless energy and indefatigable zeal performed an incalculable service for the social as well as the religious life of the West.

It was among the Methodists and Cumberland Presbyterians especially that the camp-meeting became a mighty instrument for quickening the religious life of the frontiers. That the camp-

[1] *Minutes of Methodist Conference*, 1800, 1805.

[2] "From that day Methodism grew stronger, its doctrines more popular, and its influence much greater upon all classes of society. Their persecutors became their friends."—McFerrin, *History of the Methodists in Tennessee*, I, 378.

meeting accomplished much good is undoubted. Of the earlier meetings, the physician Ramsay wrote:

> The effects of these camp-meetings were of a mixed nature. They were doubtless attended for improper purposes by a few licentious persons and by others with a view of obtaining a handle to ridicule all religion. . . . . The free intercourse of all ages and sexes under cover of the night and the woods was not without its temptations. It is also to be feared that they gave rise to false notions of religion by laying too much stress on bodily exercises, and substituting them in place of moral virtues or inward piety. These were too often considered as evidences of a change of heart and affections, though they neither proved or disproved anything of the kind. After every deduction is made of these several accounts, it must be acknowledged that the good resulting from the camp-meeting greatly preponderated over the evil. They roused that indifference to the future destiny of man which is too common, and gave rise to much serious thoughtfulness on subjects confessedly of the most interesting nature. . . . . Much of the extraordinary fervor which produced camp-meetings has abated and they are seldomer held and when held are attended by smaller numbers than formerly.[1]

The extravagances which characterized the earlier meetings bred in the Presbyterians and Baptists an aversion to such gatherings, and they were not extensively employed by those denominations. To the Methodists, however, the attendant disorders were but the accompaniment of

[1] Ramsay, *History of South Carolina*, II, 36, note.

a greater good. They saw in the institution an opportunity to reach and impress the people that no other meeting afforded. Their task was to reduce the intemperance and immorality, which had been all too prevalent in the early camp-meetings, to a minimum, while developing the possibilities for good. In 1811, Bishop Asbury wrote:

> Our camp-meetings, I think, amount to between 400 and 500 annually, some of which continue for the space of six or eight days. . . . . On such occasions many become the subjects of a work of grace, many experience much of the sanctifying influence of the Holy Spirit. Backsliders are restored, and the union of both preacher and people is greatly increased.

From the time of the Great Revival of 1800, camp-meetings have been extensively employed by the Methodists. They have been instrumental in keeping alive the spirit of vital piety, so characteristic of the denomination as a whole. Though the advisability of holding such meetings in or near the towns is an open question, they have been of great value in the frontier communities where the people, scattered over a wide area, were out of the reach of the usual channels of worship. The developed camp-meeting of today, with its regular grounds, assembly hall, cottages, and tents for the accommodation of guests, has in many instances educational features unknown to the earlier gatherings. The evolution of the camp-meeting offers an interesting field of study to the student of the religious forces of the United States.

The marked missionary spirit which prevailed in the United States at the beginning of the nineteenth century was, in large measure, due to the Great Revival of 1800 which gave new life to missionary enterprise. True, it was a part of the universal missionary movement, noted in the British Isles and on the Continent. In a sermon before the Massachusetts Baptist Missionary Society, in 1803, Samuel Stillman, pastor of the First Baptist Church of Boston, referred to "the surprising *missionary spirit* that prevails in the old world and in the new" as "one of the signal events of the present day." He continues, "Great attempts have been made and large sums of money have been, by our pious friends in Europe, expended for the important purpose of sending the gospel to pagan countries."[1] Of the work along these lines in the last years of the eighteenth and first years of the nineteenth century (a period of eight or ten years), it was said in 1804, "to exhibit an abridged detail of what has been performed within that time would require a volume."[2]

[1] Stillman, *Discourse before the Massachusetts Baptist Missionary Society* (1803), 5.

[2] Livingston, *Sermon before the New York Missionary Society* (April, 1804), 42.

The needs of the Indians and the settlers west of the mountains had been a subject of concern to the Colonial churches. In this work of evangelizing the Indians, the Moravians took the lead. Connecticut early felt the missionary impulse, and in 1774 the General Association of that colony "voted in favor of raising funds and sending missionaries to 'ye Settlements now forming in the wilderness to the Western and Northwestward'; i. e., in New York and Vermont." The Revolution interfered with these plans, and though a number of missionaries were sent out, it was not until June, 1798, that the General Association organized itself as a missionary society.[1] The Society for Propagating the Gospel among the Heathen and Others in North America had been formed in Boston in 1787.

The Dutch Reformed church after the year 1789 took up an annual collection to support missionaries on the frontiers and in Upper Canada. Collections were taken for the same purpose in the Episcopal church, from the year 1792, each state making its own decision as to the distribution of these funds.[2] Reference has already been made to the work begun by the Presbyterians in 1789,[3]

[1] Walker, *A History of the Congregational Churches in the United States*, 311, 312.

[2] "Sketch of Modern Missions," *Weekly Recorder*, August 23, 1816.

[3] P. 25.

Results of the Revival

and to the work carried on by the Methodist itinerant. These were but the prelude to the mighty modern missionary movement just referred to.

In 1796, the New York Missionary Society was organized by the Baptists and Presbyterians, inspired largely by the zeal of the London Society organized in 1795. Three years later the Northern Missionary Society in the state of New York was formed.[1] In the same year the Missionary Society of Connecticut, already referred to,[2] came into existence. Then followed, in quick succession, the Missionary Society of Massachusetts (1799), the Missionary Society of Hampshire in Massachusetts (1800), the Missionary Society of New Jersey (1801), the Baptist Missionary Society of Massachusetts (1802), and the Western Missionary Society, formed by the synod of Pittsburgh (1802). By the latter date, the work among the Presbyterians had increased to such an extent that the missionary interests were delegated to a standing committee, chosen by the General Assembly. Many other societies were formed east and west of the mountains, among them a Baptist Missionary Society in Kentucky, and a society in eastern Tennessee. In June, 1810, the American Board of Commissioners for Foreign Missions began purely foreign missionary work. The Presbyterians and

[1] These two united for foreign mission work in 1817.
[2] P. 152.

the Dutch Reformed church in 1812 and 1816 joined forces with this Congregational movement.

The field of labor of the majority of these societies was the region visited by the Great Revival of 1800 and the newer settlements farther west. The needs of the frontier had been made manifest by that movement as never before. It was impossible to supply the demands for preaching. The revival spirit had infused missionary zeal into the people west of the mountains, and societies in different localities sought to evangelize the Indians and to preach the gospel to the newer settlements along the Mississippi and north of the Ohio River. The faithful Methodist itinerant followed the emigrant farther west. The Cumberland Presbyterians and the New Lights early engaged in missionary enterprise. The Baptists and Presbyterians, too, had a share in the work among the Indians and others.

Missionary publications[1] became numerous as the work increased, and, by reports of what had

[1] The *New York Missionary Magazine and Repository of Religious Intelligence* claims to be the first of these publications in this country (Introduction, I [1800], 1-5):

"Many serious persons have lately expressed a regret, that no publication, devoted to the conveyance of religious intelligence, exists in the United States. While the presses throughout the union are teeming with literary and political journals, they have lamented that no convenient medium is found for conveying to the public information relative to the state of the Church, and the prosperity or decline of that kingdom whose interests

Results of the Revival

already been accomplished, stimulated a desire to do even greater things.

Philanthropic societies for various purposes date from this period. Mite societies among the women sprang up in different parts of the country.

they esteem more than those of any temporal sovereignty. This deficiency is the more to be regretted, as, from the scattered state of our American churches over an immense territory, communication between them is rendered difficult, if not next to impracticable, by any ordinary means. . . . . some of the most interesting articles of information, respecting the displays of Divine power in the conversion of sinners, and the promulgation of evangelical truth among the heathen in our own land, have been altogether unknown among ourselves, until they reached us through the medium of foreign publications.

"Were the present a period of ordinary aspect, perhaps there would not be so much reason to lament the want of such a channel of public intelligence. But it is far otherwise. On the one hand, the unusual prevalence of error, infidelity, and profaneness . . . . on the other, the plans which have been recently set on foot, both in Europe and America, for spreading the gospel, and which have received such unexampled support. . . . . Nor is this all: we learn from the most respectable and authentic sources that a spirit of awakening and of sanctification is poured out from on high, in copious measures, in several parts of the United States—that the number of converts to the cross of Christ seems to be increasing—and that additions are daily making to the Church (in some instances from those who were lately her bitterest enemies), of such as there is reason to hope, in a judgment of charity, will be saved.

"The work is designed to embrace, and convey to the public, every species of interesting religious intelligence. The proceedings of the three very respectable Missionary Societies which have been formed in the United States, and such as may hereafter be formed, will claim our first attention. . . . ."

Their contributions to missionary enterprise aided materially in carrying on the work of spreading the gospel. Efforts were made to supply the new settlements with Bibles, and Bible societies became important factors in the religious life of the West. Local societies were formed east and west of the mountains. In 1816, this work was furthered by the formation of the American Bible Society. Tract societies were established in New England in 1814 and in New York in 1817. Rev. Heman Humphrey, in his *Revival Sketches* published in 1859, wrote as follows:

> Thus the glorious cause of religion and philanthropy has advanced, till it would require a space which cannot be afforded in these sketches, so much as to name the Christian and humane societies which have sprung up all over the land within the last forty years. Exactly how much we at home and the world abroad are indebted for these organizations . . . . to the revivals of 1800, it is impossible to say, though much anyway."[1]

The influence of the Great Revival upon the problem of slavery is too important to remain unnoticed. While no general emancipating movement developed, the number of manumissions increased under the influence of the great excitement. The earlier movements for emancipation among the Baptists, Methodists, and Presbyterians had culminated before the beginning of the revival, though many members of these denomi-

[1] Humphrey, *Revival Sketches*, 203.

nations still unhesitatingly denounced the system and their preachers labored earnestly with slaveholders to persuade them to free their slaves. The revival intensified this spirit. One of the leaders, Barton W. Stone, made the statement that "this revival cut the bonds of many poor slaves, and this argument speaks volumes in favor of the work."[1] The Baptists in Kentucky had been the first to agitate for emancipation in the new territory. The uncompromising attitude of some of the leaders and their desire to exclude from fellowship all slaveholders led to a separation in 1805. A number of ministers and churches in the Elkhorn, North District, and Bracken associations separated or were expelled from these associations on account of slavery in that year. They called themselves "Friends to Humanity," but were generally known as "Emancipators."[2] In 1807, they organized under the name of the "Baptized Licking-Locust Association, Friends to Humanity." This became an abolition society at its next meeting.[3] Manumissions induced by this movement

[1] *Autobiography of Barton W. Stone* in Rogers, *The Cane Ridge Meeting-House*, 165: "I had emancipated my slaves from a sense of duty." (A journey to South Carolina in 1797 brought him face to face with slavery in its worst form and "was the exciting cause of my abandonment of slavery" [*ibid.*, 144, 146].)

[2] Benedict, *A General History of the Baptist Denomination in America*, II, 245-47.

[3] *Ibid.*, 248.

and by the revival probably account for the 150 per cent increase in manumissions between 1800 and 1810 noted by James G. Birney when comparing that period with the previous decade.[1]

The Great Revival was also instrumental in stirring up a sentiment against the use of intoxicating liquors which had proved so detrimental to the individual and community in many places. During this era an active campaign was entered upon which steadily gained strength in the succeeding years.

It is probable, too, that the great freedom in religious thinking, prevalent at the present day,

[1] Birney, *James G. Birney and His Times*, 23. The Emancipating Baptists sought fellowship with the Miami Association, which had been anti-slavery from the beginning. In 1804 "a letter and messengers were received from the North Bend Association in Kentucky requesting correspondence, but this was declined. Though the minutes of the Association do not state the reasons, they were doubtless founded on the practice of slavery. On this account there was never any regular correspondence between the Miami Association and any others in the Slave States, with the exception of a temporary correspondence with a small body of anti-slavery Baptists in Nelson County, Kentucky." A second attempt to open correspondence was made in 1810 and was again refused by the Miami Association. "The latter could not justify slavery so far as to correspond with those who held slaves in any manner, though avowedly, and no doubt sincerely, advocates of gradual emancipation."—Dunlevy, *History of Miami Baptist Association*, 37, 49, 50. The Baptists in the Miami valley, seem to have been affected very little by the revival. The Association records merely mention it, noting "that in the Carpenter's Run Church there were some instances of the falling exercises" (*ibid.*, 46).

owes something to the demand made by many of the revivalists that each individual be allowed to interpret the Scriptures for himself. Though their logical interpretation of the Scriptures was decidedly dogmatic in its expression, and is far removed from the idea which prevails at the beginning of the twentieth century, the latter is seen to be linked to the former when the evolutionary process is carefully considered.

Although the fervor of the revival movement abated about the year 1805, the influences it brought to bear upon the individual and the community were of a more lasting character. The forces set in motion must be reckoned with as important factors in the development of western society in the years that followed.

APPENDIXES

APPENDIX I

JAMES MCGREADY—TESTIMONY OF NINIAN EDWARDS BEFORE A COMMITTEE APPOINTED BY THE TRANSYLVANIA PRESBYTERY,[1] FEBRUARY 12, 1807.

"From a knowledge I have of James McGready since the year 1799, having since that period lived within about two miles of him and for some years of the time adjoining him being his nearest neighbor as I believe, I have been clearly of Opinion that he was one of the most honest men and possessed and practised the most exemplary piety of any man I ever saw or was acquainted with he appeared to me to be more abstracted from the things of the world and more devoted to religion uniformly than any man whose conduct I had as particularly Observed. . . . . his conduct has made such an impression on my mind that I have frequently and as sincerely declared I would rather have his chance of future happiness than any man's I ever saw."[2]

[1] Alleged that James McGready and his brother Israel had attempted to defraud the creditors of the latter—a house and lot in Russelville given James McGready in trust for his daughter being in question. The committee exonerated McGready.

[2] Mss Minutes of Transylvania Presbytery.

APPENDIX II

The Revival of 1800—One of the Favorite Hymns, "Mercy of God"[1]

Thy mercy, my God, is the theme of my song,
The joy of my heart, and the boast of my tongue:
Thy free grace alone, from the first to the last,
Hath won my affection, and bound my soul fast.

Without thy sweet mercy, I could not live here;
Sin soon would reduce me to utter despair;
But through thy free goodness my spirits revive,
And He that first made me still keeps me alive.

Thy mercy is more than a match for my heart,
Which wonders to feel its own hardness depart.
Dissolved by thy goodness, I fall to the ground,
And weep to the praise of the mercy I've found.

The door of thy mercy stands open all day
To the poor and the needy, who knock by the way;
No sinner shall ever be empty sent back
Who comes seeking mercy for Jesus's sake.

Thy mercy in Jesus exempts me from hell;
Its glories I'll sing, and its wonders I'll tell:
'Twas Jesus, my Friend, when he hung on the tree,
Who opened the channel of mercy for me.

Great Father of mercies, thy goodness I own,
And the covenant love of thy crucified Son:
All praise to the Spirit, whose witness divine
Seals mercy, and pardon, and righteousness mine.

[1] James Gallaher, *The Western Sketch Book*, 35.

APPENDIX III

[A copy of a letter from Ebenezer H. Cummins to his friend in Augusta; dated 7th of July 1802, in which is contained a true account of a great Meeting held in the district of Spartanburgh, South Carolina.][1]

ABBEVILLE, S.C., 7th July 1802

MY FRIEND,

I have just returned from Nazareth, where I have been and heard things, which no tongue can tell, no pen can paint, no language can describe, or of which no man can have a just conception until he has heard, seen and felt. I am willing that you should have a perfect detail of all the circumstances atending this Meeting; and of all the occurrences which there took place. But you must here accept the acknowledgements of my inadquacy to draw a just representation; yet as far as I may be able, I will now give you an account of some things.

The Meeting was appointed some months since by the Presbytery and commenced on Friday the 2nd instant. The grove wherein the camp was pitched was near the waters of Tyger river; and being in a vale which lay between two hills gently inclining towards each other, was very suitably adapted to the purpose. The first day was taken up in encampment until two oclock, when divine service commenced with a sermon by the Rev'd. Jno. B. Kennedy. He was succeeded by the Rev'd. William Williamson in an address explanatory of the nature and consequences of such meetings. The assembly was then dismissed. After some short time, service commenced again with a sermon by the Rev'd. James Gilleland; who was followed by the Rev'd.

[1] *Augusta Herald*, Wednesday, July 28, 1802.

Robert Wilson in a very serious and solemn exhortation. Afterwards the evening was spent in singing and praying alternately. About sun-down, people was dismissed to their respective tents. By this time the countenances of all began to be shaded by the clouds of solemnity and to assume a very serious aspect. At ten o'clock two young men were lying speechless, motionless and sometimes to all appearances, except in the mere act of breathing, dead. Before day, five others were down; these I did not see. The whole night was employed in reading and commenting upon the word of God; and also in singing, praying and exhorting, scarcely had the light of the morning sun dawned on the people, ere they were engaged in what may be called family worship. The adjacent tents collecting in groups, here and there, all round the whole line. The place of worship was early repaired to, by a numerous throng. Divine worship commenced at eight by one of the Methodist brethren, whom I do not now recollect. He was followed by the Rev'd. Shackleford, of the Baptist profession. Singing, praying and exhorting, by the Presbyterian clergymen continued until two o'clock when an intermission of some minutes was granted, that the people might refresh themselves with water, &c. By this time, the audience became so numerous, that it was impossible for all to croud near enough to hear one speaker; although, the ground rising about the stage theatrically, afforded aid to the voice. Hence, the assembly divided, and afterwards preaching was performed at two stages. An astonishing and solemn attention in the hearers, and an animating and energetic zeal in the speakers was now everywhere prevailing. Service commenced half after two by the Rev'd. Jno. Simpson at one stage, and at the other, by the Rev'd. James McElhenny, who were succeeded by the Rev. Francis Cummins. After these sermons, fervent praying, &c. were continued until and through the night in which time, many were stricken and numerous were brought to the ground.

The next morning (i e the Sabbath morning) a still higher, if possible, more engaged, and interesting spirit prevaded the whole grove, singing and praying echoed from every quarter until eight o'clock, when divine service commenced again at both stages before two great and crowded assemblies. The action sermons were delivered by the Rev. Robert Wilson at one stage and the Rev. William Cummins Davis at the other. I did not hear Mr. Wilson. But Mr. Davis was one of the most popular, orthodox gospel sermons that I ever heard. No sketch exhibited in words, would be adaquate to pourtray the appearance of the audience under this discourse. Imagine to your self thousands under the sense of the great possible danger, anxious to be informed in all that related to their dearest interests, in the presence of a counsellor, who, labouring with all his efforts, should be endeavouring to point out the way to security; and you may have some faint conception of this spectacle.

Thence ensued the administration of the Lord's Supper. To the communion sat down about four hundred persons. It was a matter of infinite satisfaction to see on this occasion the members of the Methodist and Presbyterian churches united; all owning and acknowledging the same God, the same Saviour, the same Sanctifier, and the same Heaven. We are sorry to add, that the Baptists refused to join, whether their objections were reasonably justifiable, we shall not presume to say.

The evening exercises, although greatly interrupted by the intemperance of the weather, progressed as usual, until about dark; when there commenced one of the most sublime, awfully interesting, and glorious scenes which could possibly be exhibited on this side of eternity. The penetrating sighs and excruciating struggles of those under exercise, the grateful exultations of those brought to a sense of their gulity condition, and to a knowledge of the way to salvation; mingled with the impressions which are naturally excited by the charms of music and the solemnities of prayer on such occasions; and to all this added the nature of the scenery, the darkness of the night, and the countenances of all the spectators, speaking in terms more expressive than language, the sympathy, the hope and the fear, of their hearts; were sufficient to bow the stubborn neck of infidelity, silence the tongue of profanity, and melt the heart of cold neglect though hard as adamant.

This scene continued through the night. Monday morning dawned big with the fate of its importance. The morning exercises were conducted as usual. About half after seven, the assembly met the ministers at the stage, and service commenced by the Rev. Moses Waddell. After which ensued, singing, exhorting and a concert of prayer. At length the business closed with an address, energetic and appropiate by the Rev. Francis Cummins. In the course of this day many were stricken, numbers of whom fell.

I cannot say, that the parting was not one of the most moving, and affecting scenes which presented itself thoroughout the whole. Families, who had never seen each other, until they met on the ground would pour forth the tears of sympathy, like streams of water, many friendships were formed, and many attachments contracted, which, although the persons may never meet again will never be dissolved.

Not one quarter of an hour before I mounted my horse to come away I saw one of the most beautiful sights which ever mortal eye beheld. It would not only have afforded pleasure to the plainest observer, but the profoundest Philoshpher would have found in it food for his imagination. The case to which I allude was the exercise of a Miss Dean, one of three sisters who fell near the close of the work.

Her reflections presented mostly, objects of pleasure to her view. But sometimes for the space of a minute she would lose them; the consequence of which was painful distress. By the very features of her face I could see, when her afflictive sensations approached, as plain as ever I saw the sun's light obscured by the over-passing of clouds. In her happy movements she awakened in my recollection, Milton's lovely picture of Eve when in a state of innocence.

Another extraordinary case occured at the very moment of departure. Two men disputing, one for, the other against the work referred their contest to a clergyman of responsibility, who happened to be passing that way. He immediately took hold of the hand of the unbeliever, and thus addressed him: If you were in your hearts desire to wait on the means of grace, God would show you the truth. You may expect mercy to visit you, but remember, my hand for it, it will cost you something; a stroke would not now come at a successless hour. Scarcely had the words dropped from his lips when the man was on the ground pleading for an interest in the Kingdom of Heaven, and begging pardon of God for his dishonoring him and the cause of religion, through unbelief. I understood the man to be a pious man, and his hesitations of a religious and conscientious kind.

Two other men who had been in the crowd, where many were lying under the operations of the work, attempted to run off. One leaving his hat in his haste ran about twenty or thirty paces, and fell on his face. His shrieks declared the terror and anguish under which he laboured. The other ran a different course about fifty yards and fell.

The number of those who were stricken could not be ascertained. But I believe it to be much greater than any one would conceive. On Sabbath night about twelve or one o'clock, I stood alone on a spot, whence I could hear and see all over the camp; and found that the work was not confined to one, two or three places, but over-spread the whole field; and in some large crowds the ground appeared almost covered. In the course of one single prayer of duration about ten minutes, twelve persons fell to the ground the majority of whom declared in terms audible and explicit, that they never prayed before.

There attended on this occasion, thirteen Presbyterian preachers (viz) Messrs. Simson, Cummins, Davis, Cunningham, Wilson, Waddell, Williamson, Brown, Kennedy, Gilleland, sen'r McElhenny, Dixon, and Gilliland, Jr.; and an unknown number of Methodist and Baptists.

The multitude on this ocasion far exceeded anything which had come under my observation. There were various conjectures of the numbers present; some allowed three, some seven, some four, some five, some six, some eight thousand. I have not been in the habit of seeing such multitudes together, and therefore do not look upon myself capable of reckoning any ways accurately on the subject. But I do candidly believe five thousand would not be a vague conjecture. The district of Spartanburgh where the meeting was held, contains not less than twelve thousand souls. Men of information who resided therein, said to one who might be travelling, the country would appear almost depopulated, and hesitated not in the least to say that at least two thirds of the inhabitants were present. Now supposing only one third to have attended from that district itself there would have been four thousand. Besided there were multitudes from the districts of Union, York, Lawrens, and Greenville. Numbers from Pembleton, Abbeville, Chester and Newbury and some from Green, Jackson, Elbert, and Franklin Counties of the state of Georgia.

Appendixes

Of carriages, the number was about two hundred, including waggons and all other carriages.

In a thinking mind an approach to the spot, engendered awful and yet pleasing reflections. The ideas which necessary struck the mind, were thousands in motion to a point, where to meet, tell, hear, see and feel the mighty power of God. Believe me, sir, no composition can exaggerate the spirit of one of these occasions although facts may be misrepresented: for a lively miniature, I refer you to an extract of a letter contained in a book lately published and entitled "Surprising Accounts." Where this expression is used, "The slain of the Lord were scattered over the fields."

To those who would obviate, ridicule and still entertain a doubt of the divinity of the work, I would reply in the language of Dr. Watts:

> "LAUGH ye profane and swell and burst,
>   With bold impiety
> Yet shall ye live forever cursed
>   And seek in vain to die.
>
> "Ye stand upon a dreadful steep,
>   And all beneath is hell
> Your weighty guilt will sink you deep
>   Where the old serpent fell.
>
> "Then you'll confess the frightful names
>   Of plagues you scorned before,
> No more shall look idle dreams,
>   Like foolish tales no more."

I cannot omit mentioning an idea expressed by Mr. Williamson. After taking a view of the general prevalency of dissipation and slothful neglect in religious affairs, he concluded saying, "These works appear like the last efforts of deity to preserve his church, and promote the cause of religion on this earth." To see the brilliancy and sublimity of this idea, we need only recur to the state of society for a few years back; especially in the southern states of United America; when and where, Satan with all his influence appeared to be let loose and was going about a roaring lion, seeking whom he might devour.

This extraordinary work carries in itself, demonstrably the truth of the christian religion. Men who fall and many there are who have paid no attention to the holy scriptures, yea even infidels of the deepest dye, cry out "their sinful fate by nature," "Their alienation from God," "and mans incapacity to satisfy the justice of the law under which stands the condemned," "and of course the absolute necessity of a Redeemer." Who receiving comfort from this last consideration, I have heard none crying for Mahomed, Brumma (Buddha), Grand Lama or Hamed; none but Christ was their healing balm, in him alone was all reliance fixed, on him alone was all dependence placed.

It would be exceedingly difficult to draw an intelligible representation of the effects of this work upon the human body. Some are more easily and gently wrought than others, some appear wholly wrapped in solitude while others cannot refrain from pouring out their whole souls in exhortations to those standing round;—different stages from mild swoons to convulsive spasms, may be seen;— The nerves are not unfrequently severely cramped;—The subjects generally exhibit appearances, as though their very hearts would burst out of their mouths;—The lungs are violently agitated and all accompanied with an helation; —They universally declare, that they feel no bodily pain at the moment of exercise, although some complain of a sore breast and the effects of the cramping, after the work is over;—The pulse of all whom I observed beat quick and regular, the extremities of the body are sometimes perceptably cold.—In short no art or desire could imitate the exercise.—No mimic would be able to do justice to the exhibition.—This demonstrates the error of the foolish supposition of its being feigned. I will conclude, my dear sir, acknowledging that all I have here written is incompetent to give you any complete idea of the work. Therefore to you and all who wish to be informed I say come, hear, see and feel.

I am yours respectfully,

EBENEZER H. CUMMINS

APPENDIX IV

[Rev. John Lyle's account of sacramental meetings at Point Pleasant and Lexington in June, 1801, Lyle Diary, 3, 4, 9-20.]

a) SACRAMENTAL MEETING AT POINT PLEASANT

June 29, 1801, Mr. Howe administered the sacraments at Pleasant Point on Stoner. The number that attended computed to be 3 or 4000 several waggons and carriages and stages. [Mr. Lyle among the ministers present on this occasion.] The people were engaged in singing and hearing and praying night and day from friday morning to Tuesday evening. The numbers that fall down were great. I do not know how many, some say 300—I made no calculation. Some old men fell, some young ones of robust constitution, some children about 11 (as ———) about 7 or 8 (as ———'s two children) One ——— fell who was telling his daughters lying in distress that if they would again come to such meetings he would beat them well. He fell with these words in his mouth. One ——— said to a neighbor that he feared the work was not right. He fell as if shot but was drunk a day or two after at meeting. Two Miss ———'s were struck down one had opposed the work bitterly that morning, one lay as if near dead about 2 or three hours but had a high pulse. The other when I spoke to her said Jesus had led her in a way she knew not seemed awfully serious but some comforted. It would fail to say something on every case. Some lay as if about to expire in a few moments. Some gron'd and breathed and wrought hard, as in the agonies of death. Some shrieked as if pierced to the heart with a sword on account of their hardness of heart and insensibility as Mrs. ———, a great variety appeared but the chief distress of mind was sin and guilt and blindness, unbelief and hardness of heart &c. or they were overwhelmed with joy or fainting and thirsting for the presence of Christ. I never heard such earnest inquiry after Christ as on Monday."

b) SACRAMENTAL MEETING AT LEXINGTON THE LAST SABBATH OF JUNE, 1801

"A few facts respecting the Sacrament at Lexington last Sabbath of June. I had been solicited to assist Mr. Welsh before I heard of the sacrament at Indian Creek near Cynthiana. When I went to Lexington on Saturday I seemed to envy those that were gone there for I thought we would have a very uncomfortable meeting because. br. Howe, Stone and Marshall and their people were chiefly gone to Cynthiana, my young people either went there or staid at home to hear a Methodist who preached at Salem. Mr. Crawford's young people were there on Saturday and Sunday, but on Monday saw none of the Thompsons or McDonals. Mr. Blythe's young people many of them were gone to Cynthiana. On Saturday Mr. Stuart and I preached, no falling down. On Sunday, Mrs. ——— fell about 11 o'clock and produced a great curiosity among the people. She was delivered spoke (though with some nervous agitation and some wildness of countenance) of a glorious deliverance from distress, clouds and darkness. She said she had heaven in possession begun below &c. I asked her what views she had of herself—she said she was poor and wretched she was nothing but she had great hopes in Jesus of the happiness in the world to come. She asked her friends to go with her, what says she, but one pilgrim going alone, Oh, come and go along &c., &c. The people pressed, crowded and seemed generally curious to see and hear. A few acquaintances were much affected. Next a Miss ——— that fell at Salem fell and was carried to a log at some distance from the tent when I came there the curious multitude pressed hard upon us and no keeping them off. [Miss] ——— also fell and became speechless. Mrs. Nicholas relic of the late Colonel Nicholas came with vinegar and bread and rub'd their faces and noses and put it in their mouths. This hurt the feelings of the (I hope pious) but as to the bodily effects ignorant people they insisted she should not apply these medicines for they thought these bodily effects some apendage which could not be cured in this way. She ordered the rubbing of her hands, &c. ———'s sister at length pushed her away. She went to Miss ——— and was putting vinegar on her. ——— was not wholly speechless. She told her it would do her no good. Mrs. Nicholas said it would unless she was a hypocrite and that she appeared very like one for her face was rather ruddy for one in a fainting fit. This wounded the friends. ——— began to fall. I took her away. She was weakened and agitated with distress because of the opposition that was made by Mrs. Nicholas and others. When I came back, Miss ———, a sister of the other was fallen and speechless. I went up to the tent to hear Mr. Stevenson of South Carolina preach. He made a delightful sermon on not by works of righteous. which we have done &c. Titus &c. When sermon was over I went to lodge at Mr. Blythe's. Sunday evening held society in the meeting house. Mr. Blythe and myself spoke and then the people began to sing. Just after exhorting was over one elder fell down but when we got to him was not speechless. I asked what was the matter if he found himself a sinner, yes he said what he never before believed to be a reality He found himself to be a great sinner. He deeply groaned but talked sensibly. I prayed

Appendixes 177

for him at his request &c. He told his friends it was reality
&c. Mr Bradly says this man had told ——— ——— that
if he fell he might put his foot on his neck and keep him
down. I went from him to go to the pulpit but on my road
saw a commotion in the assembly. I went there, found
——— ——— and an old fellow trying to influence the minds
of the people by crying out that there were ladies in distress
who had no friends. I went and talked to the young lady,
a Miss ———. She expressed a sense of sin and danger
&c [word uncertain] but not fallen down. ——— was at
my left hand as he was talking I asked him his name—
He drew his fist and said he was a man. I asked him again
as politely as I could his name. He said he was a man.
I asked what he wanted he said he wanted to take those
ladies to the air who had no friends. I told him I was
a friend to the ladies, he doubted it from my conduct. I
asked what conduct. He said don't provoke me to speak
my mind. I told him that I was not afraid for I had the
testimony of my conscience. He said I was as infernal
scoundrel. I told him he did not hurt me by saying so.
Well said he, I will do something to hurt you. I asked
what for, he said you have hindered the ladies of fresh air.
I said I had but just come and had not. Then says he I am
a liar. If you call me a liar I'll whip or be whipped (Mr.
Stuart tried to calm him) I told him to ask them if they
wanted fresh air. He told me to put the question. I asked
the lady if she wanted air she said no. . . . . I went into
a seat where a Miss ——— was lying. I asked what was
the matter—Ah says she, I don't know I never was so
before. I little thought when I came here to be this way.
I said dont you see that you have sinned against God and
have you no load of guilt upon your mind. Oh yes says
she enough of it. I have been a great sinner. Oh I shall
never get over it in the world. I can never be saved. At

times she would apply a vial of hartshorn and complain of a weight in her breast and something in her hands. She said she would never get away from that place. All I could [say] about Christ and salvation could have no effect that I could distinctly perceive to quiet her mind. I went to two afterwards that were lying before the pulpit. One a young lady complained of sin &c. but seemed more sensible and seemed in a more hopeful way than Miss ———. The other was a young man who thought he had religion before but I believe had doubted— I went to ———'s daughter who was almost speechless, but could say she had fallen through a sense of sin. I then went home to Mr. Blythe's about eleven o'clock or twelve, the people staid till almost two. When I got near the tent on Monday I was met by a company bringing away a man who said he had found Christ gracious to his soul &c. (had been seeking two years). I talked to him and prayed for him, his wife seemed much affected. I addressed the audience around on the subject of curiously prying into their own hearts, &c. I went to the tent. Mr. Stevenson had begun the service. He preached on this text, In the world ye shall have tribulation but be of good cheer I have &c. Some were down, I believe when he began. Shortly after———'s son fell and was carried off upon the hill, where a company gathered. Presently a Miss ——— of Georgetown, screamed out three or four times a great and bitter cry, the audience was for a minute all in motion. She soon began to address her brother in an affectionate manner and prayed to the lord aloud— I told her Christ was near, she became pacified. I got the people to stand back and take seats and returned to the stand. This Miss ——— broke into raptures about Jesus. When I began to preach on Isa. 45:22. There were several down, one on the stage at my feet to the right and two down before the tent &c. I prayed against enthusiasm and in my sermon gave marks of true illumination and true faith mentioned the parable of the Tares, exhorted them to guard against enthusiasm &c. that it like a worm destroyed the beauty of a revival and would ere long discredit the work of God. I said people and ministers might go wrong, refered to the history of Whitfield's day &c, &c. Davenport's extractions respecting himself and those who followed him. Mr. Crawford was very busy among the people the time I was preaching except little intervals said many were comfortably exercised and that he got on wing &c. I even spoke to the people to be as quiet as possible and reproved the wanderers. Many were going up the hill to hear a class leader one Murphy exhort. . . . . I had I hope clearness and liberty in describing faith and giving the general invitation and found that my sermon was very pleasing to men who might be pious, but were afraid of enthusiasm being in the work. I found also that it was pleasing to many others but some thought it might open the mouths of opposers to speak against the work because of the caution made against enthusiasm. The Lord hath it in His own hand and so the opposers. I hope I am in some measure engaged to promote my Redeemer's kingdom and not striving to be the greatest. In the sermon I preached on Song. 5. 16 Yea he is altogether lovely. I seemed to aim at the glory of Jesus. But to return after sermon the work went on rapidly. Many fell and agonized and groaned under the sense of sin, and many I hope were delivered and rejoiced with trembling. The first I went to see was old ———'s wife, she was agonizing under a sense of sin and hardness of heart and wanted Christ. She got more comfortable views after some hours but expressed herself modestly—appeared joyful but in no extasy. I went to where the widow ———'s son, of Blue Spring and daughter lay and ———'s daughter and a Miss ———

and a Miss ——— and I think one or two more. They lay in about a rod or half a rod square. Mr. ——— was deeply affected, some nervous agitations but could speak, He had to all appearance a very deep sense of sin and Miss———, his sister seemed in a recovering way but very weak, she spoke but little. After some time I saw them come out of the crowd. He talked a good deal about Christ being gracious to his soul, was still weeping and agitated, perhaps partly on account of sinners. She seemed more serene and modestly professed deliverance. Miss ——— seemed to express a deep sense of sin. Miss ——— had been down, what the cause of her now falling I do not recollect, but she expressed a confidence in Christ. Miss——— of Walnut Hill was sorely wrought in frightful nervous agitations, was incapable of conversing till near night. When she was put in the carriage she was able to converse and expressed her sense of sin and hope of mercy through the Lord Jesus. I talked with her next day. She had hope and comfort, but not fully satisfied. One ———, who lives on Mr. Welsh's place fell. He said he had struggled against falling for three hours but was brought down at last. He complained much of sin and danger and hardness, unbelief, etc. But had comfortable feelings that evening I hope in Christ. ——— and Mr. ———'s prentice, a large young man, fell and lay powerless for some time under a deep sense of sin and danger &c. Had the use of speech. I would here remark, Doctor Warfield sent me a vial of hartshorn which I faithfully used without success in any case that I know of. ——— was lying flat on his back and unfortunately some ran in his nostrils but he did not seem to feel it though he could talk of sin &c. So much were his thoughts taken up with other subjects. His hands felt cold as were the hands of several. Their pulse is low in that case; but sometimes the pulse is full as in health but
/

more quick (opinor). Sometimes the pulse is so weak and the nerves so tremulous that you can not feel a pulse at all without great care. Sometimes the face flushes with a pale red as in the case of a Miss ——— on Sunday. ——— I heard was down, I went and asked what was the matter. She said she was overcome by the goodness of God. Afterwards she told that she had on Friday to give up all hope, thought she had no religion and would never get away. But had got a happy deliverence, seemed serene and joyful but weeped. She said when the people came about her she was not able to tell what they meant, until she made an exertion and found her power was gone. She seemed sweetly engaged all that evening. Mr. ———, ——— and I don't know how many more fell agonizing for sinners and what generally raises them is a hope that God will convert sinners, or else they are enabled to resign them into the hands of God to do as seemeth him good. When in distress they seem in a nervous agony and complain of some times unbelief and hardness of heart as did ———: I have now gone through with most cases I saw and remember (perhaps little ———, Mrs. ———'s neice is not mentioned who seemed as rationally convinced as almost any of them.) There were some affected much who did not quite fall as ———, ——— and ——— her father. Many who fell were strangers and many probably I neither saw nor heard of. It was tho't by Gen. Robt. Todd that there were fifty fell. I can count about 35 that came under my notice but there might be more than as many more, for what I know. ——— fell at Salem and many times since fell again. On Monday I rode in the carriage to hold her as we came from the tent to Col. Patterson's she was pale and speechless her hands cold and her pulse weak and her body limber. When she came to she told us the cause of the last fall was this, a little girl of the name of Gibson and she had got acquainted on the occasion and they were mightily taken up together when she came Miss Gibson professed a great attachment to [her] and she fell down because her affections were so mov'd she could not stand it. I asked if she did not feel guilt and dispair when she first fell &c. If a less degree of distress did not throw her down yesterday than ever before—she said yes. I asked if she had not a want of appetite and her body weaker than before—she said yes. I asked if she did not find that resignation raised her up. I gave advise as in the case [of] White &c.

APPENDIX V

[Rev. John Lyle's account of the great Cain Ridge camp meeting, August, 1801, Lyle Diary, 21-35.]

Cain Ridge 2d. sabbath 8th August, 1801 Arrived yesterday evening . . . . heard that Mr. Houston had preached on Friday and Mr. Howe was preaching when we came. I held society at Andrew Irvines that evening. Saturday preached on Mat. 4.2. . . . . Had not much liberty the people were pretty attentive but no falling or crying out that I perceived. In the afternoon McNamar preached on Rom I am not ashamed of the Gospel of Christ— He preached us a discourse unintelligible to myself and others with whom I conversed about it. But it contained the substance of what Mr. Stone and he call the true new gospel which they say none preach but ourselves. He spoke of the Gospel bringing a pardon with it, and talks the design of it is to bring persons to self despair at once. The scheme is antinomian as in Marshal on Sanctification and Armenian in some degree about faith &c, &c. I know it not. But I humbly hope I understand the Gospel of Jesus. . . . . McNamar . . . . lively in desultory exhortation and speaks and sings with all his power and in address much like a Methodist. He sometimes rises to extatic joy—it smiles through his face division has resulted in his church. I expect the conduct of these hot-headed men and the effect of their doctrine will separate the church of Christ and quench the revival &c. Saturday evening the people crowded the meeting house. Some fell down. I saw Mr. McNamar here praying, when the women's voices for whom he was praying appeared to be the highest and many others singing, praying and groaning all around some rejoicing and some crying for mercy. He might better have prayed silently for the person. I traversed the camp and then went to Captain Venable's tent and took a nap. I rose before day and went to where lawyer———— had fallen and rose again and was talking to the people. He said he fell because of his coldness and deadness &c, but rose revived and happy. I traversed the camp in the morning. Went into the meeting house found Houston exhorting. After he had done I spoke on love to God and man on the Christian character as exemplified by our Saviour in his life. It rained very hard for some hours. At the tent Mr. Marshal preached the action sermon. Arise my fair one and come away &c. I heard a little of it and then went to the meeting house and found it full and then to where Mr. Burke was preaching to a large audience. Many of them appeared to be Methodists, they shouted before he was done, but afterwards they shook hands and got into a singing extacy. There was a great shaking of hands and praying and exhorting. Mr. McNamar exhorted the people not to oppose but to come and taste the love of God &c, &c. He seemed much affected. I went in among a cluster of rejoicers and shook hands with some of them, one stood staring like he saw Christ in the air, I asked him what views he had of Christ. He said he saw a fullness in him for all that come. Their looks were joyful but their appearance rather light but I cannot describe it. I went from them to the Communion, and sat down at the first table which Mr. Blythe served. I had some reviving clearer views of divine things than I had before. In time the tables were serving Mr. Samuel Finley preached on how shall we escape if we neglect so great salvation. I heard a part of that and then went to serve tables. When I spoke I felt uncommonly tender &c.

There were eleven hundred communicants, according to the calculation of one of the elders others say better than eight hundred. After the communion Mr. Blythe took me aside, we were talking about disorder, the danger of enthusiasm etc. and Mr. Marshall came and told us ——— had fallen. We went to him, he complained that he was a great sinner, had a hard heart &c. But appeared confounded, said it was an unfortunate sight, a great mortification. He prayed and asked others to pray for him. After an hour or so he rose and went to the woods but seemed more light on Monday than might be expected. Tuesday he seemed to have a deeper sense of the hardness of his heart. But to return, I felt much melted when I saw the rebel down, tears flowed in abundance. Blythe and Welsh wept, but Blythe immoderately. That evening when we returned there was a shout in the Camp of Israel. Many were falling and rising and rejoicing &c. &c. Several of Mr. Houston's people were down, and one or two rejoicing. I turned into praying and exhorting among them, as did other ministers and continued I suppose near to one or two o'clock. I prayed for and talked to several that were standing and for Mrs. ——— who was fallen and got relief at that place. She had been under conviction for two or three months. After some time I went up into the stand and found five or six (who I supposed had gone there to see the work) fallen. There were ———'s daughters near Lexington, one Henderson and one Barry. If I recollect right one of them seemed to get comfort that night. How it fair'd with the rest I don't know. Also I talked with two Miss ———'s and ———, Col. ———'s daughter from Elkhorn, the last got comfort though at first in despair several wept around. I went around and through the meeting house, found many asleep in their seats and some down but not much stir in the house—some out of doors were praying &c. and some down. I went where a negro was preaching and after he was done exhorted and went to Mr. Venable's tent and lay down. In the course of this imperfect and very concise narrative I only mention those I knew and whose names I heard and do remember. The number of those whose names I knew not I cannot tell. Next morning I arose about or before the break of day and retired to the woods—as I returned I saw two young men down, I think they said relations to James Crockets family. They were incapable of conversing and seemed in great distress. I then went to ———'s tent and prayed for Mrs. ———'s sister [her husband] I understood had been down twice. After breakfast I went to the meeting house and employed Mrs. Rite to help me out with the fallen that the house might not be so crowded and sultry. But before this I went to the meeting house and Mr. Tull was preaching, I exhorted after he prayed and then he exhorted and I prayed and he exhorted again and set the people to sing Come ye sinners &c. ——— fell down and sent for me. He seemed much affected and agitated and seemed to doubt his religion he got among the Baptists. His wife came and fell on him and cry'd but he told me is yet opposed to the work. She would not even shake hands with her sister-in-law when she lay rejoicing &c. One and another fell down and the work went on briskly. Then after breakfast I went to talk with an old Mrs. Ramseys son who was rejoicing and heard Robert Campbell come and tell one Dooly that Robert Finley was speaking—says he, He is a worthy speaker. I went down and heard him speak, but he soon concluded. I exhorted the people a while and went to the meeting house and began to carry out the people and continued to carry out and pray and exhort till the middle of the day or about one o'clock During this time I heard a number of those that were delivered arise and speak for their friends and the people and numbers got convicted and fell down. Their orations consist of the plain and esential truths of the gospel that they themselves have been powerfully convinced of, but they speak them with all the feeling and pathos that human nature affected with the most important objects is capable of. They speak much of the fullness of Christ, his willingness to save &c. Among the rest we carried out a man that had been convulsed very much indeed so that you might have heard his feet strike the floor for many yards. He when carried out appeared joyful but weak. He would say, Bless the Lord, but nothing else. Sometime after I was sent for and met the Governor who said that he was gone distracted, that his head was weak before &c. I went to hear Mr. Rankin from Logan preach—he preached a plain sermon about conviction and conversion &c. After he was done Northcut, the Methodist exhorted. After he was done I gave a description of the heavenly city from Revelations. After dinner went down to the house again, took Fowler and McNutt and Bard and came up with Campbell of Mr. Marshal's bounds we began to talk to and pray for those that were fallen down and ——— a deist fell, a son to widow ———. He's now turned back Nov. 16. He had said just before he would not fall so for a thousand dollars and that he did not believe in heaven, hell or the devil. Shortly after two of his cousins fell. He lay speechless for an hour or two then spoke and said he had been rideculing the work before he fell and said he wanted to pray and seek Christ. This evening I talked to one Standerford who keeps tavern near the blue licks, who it was said got comfort and exhorted &c. About dusk I went into the meeting house and found ——— rejoicing and calling sinners to come to Christ. She said she had deceived herself and had never known Christ before she went up to the tent and talked to her friends, a Miss

―――― was struck down just by her and seemed much distressed. ―――― talked a great deal about the hardness of her heart and how she was delivered. By the man who held her up saying give all up into the hands of Christ &c. ―――― was relieved going home had like to have fallen from her horse. Broke out in upbraiding me for not praying for her at Salem and said I did not believe she was in earnest there. But now she could pray for herself and for me told me to come along with her she would go with me to heaven. She talked about her sin in going to the holy table of the Lord unprepared and that it would have been just in God to have sent her to hell for so great a sin. She said ―――― got comfort, she was glad because she had got one to walk with her. At other times she rejoiced but she did not know what for, but she had not found Christ. She spoke of her unworthiness and Christs fullness and his willingness to save beautifully &c. She talked almost all night. In the morning when I came away she was asleep, but I understood was verry much hurt because I went away without speaking to her. Her nerves were much affected, the veins of her neck much swell'd and she was much exhausted by speaking. ――――'s sister-in-law fell from her horse between (Patton's) and Crocketts and appeared in deep distress. The meeting at Cain Ridge continued on to Thursday we have heard and do not know whether it be yet broke or not. It was allowed a thousand had fallen before I came away and then I recon there were 60 down and they continued to fall and be exercised. The last account on Wensday I heard they were almost all men that fell on Tuesday. Tuesday morning I viewed the camp saw a number down. Went to the meeting house found a number of boys and girls singing and shaking hands, a sort of wagging that appeared like dancing at a distance. When I came among them they appeared verry loving and joyful almost dizzy with joy. I told them to sing the same hymn and not sing different ones so near together. Mr. Rankin came in I told the people we would have an address from the pulpit and to take their seats which they did immediately and he spoke first and I next the people were verry attentive and a good deal moved. Then word was given that Mr. Burke would preach at the tent or stand. He began to preach a sermon on having no continueing place and seeking a better &c. in a highly decorated style like Hervey. I left the place about half after twelve (the above paragraph is out of place as to the natural order of history) I heard of people being there on Thursday.

APPENDIX VI

THE GREAT REVIVAL IN NORTH CAROLINA—AMONG THE BAPTISTS OF THE KEHUKEE ASSOCIATION[1]

Elders Burkett and Read record a long period of darkness during which the churches appeared to be on a general decline. In some there were hardly enough members to hold conference. In some the Lord's Supper was seldom administered. Few were added by baptism for several years. In 1794 the Saturday before the fourth Sunday in every month was appointed a day of prayer-meeting for revival. A small appearance of the beginning of the work was noted in 1800. "But at the Association at Great Swamp in 1801, Elder Burkett, just returning from Tennessee and Kentucky, brought the news .... that in about eight months six thousand had given a rational account of a work of grace on their souls and had been baptized in the State of Kentucky and that a general stir had taken place amongst all ranks and societies of people: and that the work was still going on. The desirable news seemed to take such an uncommon effect on the people, that numbers were crying out for mercy, and many praising and glorifying God. Such a Kehukee Association we had never before seen. The ministers all seemed alive in the work of the Lord and every Christian present in rapturous desire was ready to cry, *Thy Kingdom Come*. The ministers and delegates carried the sacred flame home to their churches and the fire began to kindle in the greatest part of the

[1] Elders Lemuel Burkett and Jesse Read, *History of the Kehukee Baptist Association*, 138–56. Burkett and Read were ministers of the gospel in Northampton and Halifax counties, North Carolina, at the time of the Great Revival and published this account in 1803.

churches, and the work increased. The first appearance that was discovered was *great numbers of people* attended the ministry of the word, and the congregations kept increasing." In some places as many at a meeting on a common day as used to meet on a Sunday, as many on Sundays as formerly at great meetings. "The word preached was attended with such a divine power, that at some meetings two or three hundred would be in floods of tears, and many crying out loudly *what shall we do to be saved.*" Old Christians were so revived that they were all on fire to see their neighbors, their neighbors' children, and their own families so much engaged. "Many backsliders returned weeping home. . . . . The work increasing many were converted and they began to join the churches." Some churches that had not received a member by baptism in a year or two now received several at almost every conference meeting, sometimes 12, 14, 18, 20, 24 at several times in one day. Some received in the revival nearly 200 members each. In four churches lying between Roanoke and Meherrin rivers about 600 were baptized in two years. "The work has engaged the attention of all sorts of people—rich and poor, and all ranks. Many very respectable persons in character and office have been called in in this revival." A few of the churches in the Association had not as yet experienced a revival. According to accounts returned to the two last Associations 1,500 had been added by baptism to the churches in the Kehukee Association.

"The Lord was pleased to make use of weak and simple means to effect great purposes. . . . . *Singing* was attended with a great blessing; Elder Burkett published two or three different pamphlets which contained a small collection of spiritual songs, some of which he had brought from the western countries. They were in very great demand. As many as about 6,000 books were disposed of in about two years. We might truly say, *the time of the singing of birds had come, and the voice of the turtle was heard in our land.* At every meeting before the minister began to preach the congregation was melodiously entertained with numbers singing delightfully, while all the congregations seemed in lively exercises. Nothing seemed to engage the attention of the people more; and the children and servants at every house were singing these melodious songs. From experience, we think we can assure our readers that we have reason to hope that this, with other means, proved a blessing in this revival.

"*Shaking hands* while singing was a mean (though simple in itself) for to further the work. The ministers used frequently, at the close of worship, to sing a spiritual song suited to the occasion, and go through the congregation and shake hands with the people while singing; and several when relating their experience at the time of their admission into church fellowship, declared that this was the first means of their conviction. The act seemed so friendly, the ministers appeared so loving that the party with whom the minister shook hands would often be melted in tears. The Hymn

> 'I long to see the happy time,
> When sinners all come flocking home;
> To taste the riches of his love,
> And to enjoy the realms above.'

And especially that part of it,

> 'Take your companion by the hand,
> And all your children in the band,'

—many times had a powerful effect.

"*Giving the people an invitation to come up to be prayed for*, was also blessed. . . . . The ministers usually at the close of preaching, would tell the congregation that if there were any persons who felt themselves lost and condemned, under the guilt and burden of their sins, that if they would come near the stage and kneel down, they would pray for them. Shame at first kept many back but as the work increased numbers apparently under strong conviction would come and fall down before the Lord at the feet of the ministers, and crave an interest in their prayers. Sometimes twenty or thirty at a time. And at Union Meetings two or three hundred would come and try to come as near as they could. . . . . . Many ladies of quality at times were so powerfully wrought on as to come and kneel down in the dust in their silks to be prayed for.

"*Relating experiences and the administration of the ordinance of baptism* were greatly blessed in this revival. When the churches held conference to receive members (which they always did in a public assembly) the congregation would draw up in such crowds, as they would tread one on another anxious to hear the experiences of their neighbors and families. And while the candidates were relating their experience the audience would be in floods of tears and some almost convulsed while their children, companions and friends were relating their conversion. And several declared this was the means of their conviction."

Administration of baptism had a great effect—sometimes 15 or 20 would be received at one time—great numbers would attend—200 to 1,000 and more. To see fifteen or twenty persons, suitably attired to go into the water, who usually stood in a row, a small distance from the water hand in hand, and the minister joining the rank at the head "march down into the water regularly . . . . singing as they went,

'Come all ye mourning souls who seek rest in Jesus' love,
Who set your whole affection on things that are above;
Come let us join together and hand in hand go on,
Until we come to Canaan where we no more shall mourn,'

would take a solemn effect on the assembly. Numbers would be in floods of tears, and so greatly affected could scarcely stand, while they would express their sincere wishes that they were prepared to go in with their children and companions." To see father and son, mother and daughter, husband and wife go in together, hand in hand, "proved conviction to many."

"*Evening meetings* were greatly blessed." These had been disused for some time—began to revive when the revival commenced . . . . some would come ten miles to a night meeting. Usually had a sermon preached when a minister was present.

"*Union meetings* have also been attended with a blessing. An Union meeting consists of several churches, being convenient to one another of the same faith and order, who meet at stated times to confer in love about matters relating to peace, brotherly union and general fellowship." Generally held three days—incident of a former Senator from the county. When the minister concluded preaching on Sunday,[1] he rose from his seat, "stood on a bench and told the people 'that he had many times been a *candidate* at *elections*, but he was now a *candidate* for *the Kingdom of Heaven.*' And being overpowered with the love of God fell backwards off his seat, but was upholden by some of the bystanders." Nearly 1,000 present at his baptism a few weeks later. "At the side of the water he thus addressed the people, 'I perceive several of my friends and old companions standing around; and I can truly say I love you, but I cannot continue with you in the ways we have so long been in, and if you will not go with me, I must leave you,' and so bade them farewell and went into the water." August, 1803, supposed 4,000 present

[1] Union meeting held in June 1803 at Elder Henly's meeting-house in Bertie.

at Union meeting at Parker's meeting-house—service in open air—Elder Burkett preached—rain fell but the congregation still kept together—"some crying, some convulsed on the ground, some begging the ministers to pray for them."—These meetings generally blessed—effects on the people various—some though deeply affected made no noise, others in floods of tears, at last constrained to cry out in the presence of the multitude, '*What must I do to be saved?*' "Some were taken with a tremour like a fit of ague. And others fell to the ground like a person in a swoon, and continued helpless and motionless for some time; and this power was manifest at times on persons at home about their secular concerns in the house, and in the field."

The authors note the good effect of these experiences on the people and the tendency to moralize them—"Persons of the most dissolute lives, as drunkards, swearers, liars, thieves, &c, become sober, punctual, honest persons. . . . . In some neighborhoods persons at enmity with each other and when they met would not speak to one another, after receiving the benefits of the gospel's gracious influence, could take each other in their arms with the greatest pleasure."

APPENDIX VII

["An acount of the revival of relegio[n which] began in the Estern part of the state of Kentuckeye in May 1801."][1]

at a society on the waters of Fleming a Boy under 12 years got afected in an extrodinery manow publickly confesing his sins and recomending Jesus Christ to sinors several growen persons got impretions that did not ware of the flame spread into sosciteye it began under Mr Campble on sundaye at his meating house to appear more publickly —the last sunday in May on cabin creeke under M^r McNemar on a secramental ocasion about 60 persons got Struck down but the effects had appered in that congration some weekes before the saboth folowing on a like occasion on Fleming creeke und[e]r Mr Campble and M^r M^{c}nemar upwards of one hundred was struck and under deep conviction for sins on the first sabath in June M^r stone appointed the lord's super to be adminestred at Concord in the Bounds of which congration there was the above afects

[1] [By Col. Robert Patterson], *Draper MSS*, The Patterson Papers, No. 105, 3 MM. A similar but briefer letter (which contains some additional items) from Col. Robert Patterson to Rev. Dr. John King dated September 25, 1801, found in March, *Increase of Piety*, etc., pp. 35-40, has this introduction:

REV. SIR:

"By the following, I mean to communicate to you as accurate and comprehensive an account of the revival of religion at present in the eastern parts of this State [Kentucky] and round about where I live, as I am able.

"On the first of May at a society on the waters of Fleming Creek on the east side of Licking, a boy . . . . "; see also Patterson letter in *New York Missionary Magazine* for 1802.

appered at societies and preachings, the fridaye night before for the first time I was present at a society near Kainridge meating house ten mild from Concord nine fell down and was afected in the yousual way I proseeded to concord on saturday sermon began at the yousual time in which time some began to be afected and continued all night saboth was a solem day nomber got afected and fell down the lords super adminestered by Mr Stone McNemar Ja^s Craford Mr Welch Mr Rynolds the exercises continued night and day untill Wednisday about 200 got afected about 4000 people attended 12 waggons this was the first meeting that shewed the nesesety of incamping on the ground The meeting housees could not contain the people the camp was exlenonined by candles furneshed by the congration which was in a thick grove of beach timber the apperance of itselfe gave a solem apperance but ad to that preaching exorting singing praying sinors rejoicing publickly testifoying that the ware delivered from the bodage of sin and death others under deep conviction lementing that the wore dredfull sinors the whole to gether struck eavery person with a solem aw a few excepted

the lords super [was appoi]nted to be held at point plesent in one of Mr Joseph Hows congrations on the 3^d sabath of June the news had began to spread for the first time I attended with my famileye about 40 waggons 8000 people seposed to attend the meeting conti^d from fridaye to wednesdaye abot 250 people became afected the opesition began to appear more hear then it had done before the 3^d saboth in July was appointed for the lords super to be held in Lexington Mr Welches congration the same day at indian creeke Mr Robertsons congration at the later place the begun on thursday continued to thirsday folowing night and day the first night excepted 10000 people attended 50 waggons with thier fameleyes 800 got afected

Lexington comenced of fridaye[1] in the Meetinghouse on saturdaye the preaching began at a tent a mile below town at M^{c}conells spring meeting was agurned from the tent in the eavening to meet in the meeting house with candleliting continued till 12 oclock   met sabath at the stand 6000 people   the people began to be efected in the yousual way   about 70 in all was struck down   mondaye was a solem day the people left town on tusdaye   now occasion that I have been at appeared so solem and those ingaged who thought well of the woork parted under the grates appere of friendship   the minesters who began to distinguish themselves to be friends to the work was Ja^s Craford Robt Marsha[ll] Mr Lyle Stone M^{c}nemar Campble Rynolds Robertson Joseph How & Shanon Mr Blyth has not yet appeared   in the caus thier congrations lay betwixt Kentuck river and the ohio east of Kentucky river   the opisition was great on the last mentoned occasion from the dayest[2] and old nominal profesors   the reformed synod and presbetery people generaly was in opesition   the former impute it to sympethe prinsepaly the aledge from the melody of singing the most easeye to be afected gets so and others by them—the later say that it is hypockcresy inthesesim posesion of the Devil witchcraft &c

in gaveing my opinion I will describe it as [MS torn][3] not yet being a subject of that extrodenery work   I have seen of eavery age sects and description from eight years upwards   those that has been subject has been operated on diferently some has had symtoms before the fell the

[1] Being the first time this strange work made its appearance here," Patterson letter to Rev. John King, March, *Increase of Piety*, etc., p. 39).

[2] Probably *deist*.

[3] "I had it from the subjects."   Patterson letter to Rev. John King, March, *Increase of Piety*, p. 37.

Appendixes 199

have felt it in the grait arteraye of the thyes and arms but like a shock closed in emedently to the hart the hart sweels liking to burst the bodaye occasions shortness and quickness of breath the become motienless the feet and hands become cold but the pulse generaly regular the ceace breathing hard and become easaye before the can speake the heat returns to the extremety one of two subjects the talke on either that the are dredfull siner some times in a state of despere aledging that there is now salvation for them or the have got a hope of salvation through Christ and recomend Christ to sinors in the most presing manow caling on their friends to fly to christ that if the are damned it will be thier own blame that christ dyed for sinours that he is able to save the vilest sinour at that time the have graet gifts in exhorting and prayer love provails with them the get a disposition and ability to pray and that without cesing the some times hear eavery thing that is said to them the want now now no aplication of medeson alltho the wether has been verrye warm and much crouded about them yet the say the heat do not afect them[1] others feel now aproching symtoms but fall as if shot dead and do not recolect any thing untill the begin to recover which is from one hour to 24 some lay easaye without any symtoms of distress not able to speak or eaven to grone others vereye much convulsed and screams awfuly as if going to the botemliss pitt which the say is gaping for them on sacramental occon[s] the most generaly get struck as well as at sosiety at home fameleys have been wholy taken down the have fell on the road—plowing in fields in bead a sleep and awake indiveduals in fameley [ch]ildren at scool whare

[1] "They are all opposed to any medical application; and though the weather is very warm and people in large crowds around them, yet they do not incline to drink water" (Patterson letter to the Rev. John King, March, *Increase of Piety*, etc., p. 37).

now religious exercises ware going on those that ware in oposition of the on the spot and at the time in a number of instance have been struck down dayes drunkards hworemongers profain persons those that at the time ware caling it the divels woork inthuism witchcraft idolatry and methodism have been struck down and in now instance have I heard them speak on their recovery other then confess thier sins with reserve and recoment christ to sinours as above stated=

the first saboth in august was appointed for the lord super at Kain ridge congration began on friday continued untill wednisdaye 12000 people 125 waggons 8 carages 900 comunicants 300 struck a gerl aged 10 y[ears] was struck when able to speak began to exhort continued two hours in prayer and exhorting in vereye powerfull and pressing manow the 3^d saboth in august was appointed for the lords super to be held in paris burbon county Mr Rynold congration 8000 people 32 waggons 6 carages 350 comunicants 200 struck grait oposition the first sabeth in September was apointed for the Lords super at Walnuthill Mr Crafords congration seven mild south east of Lexington 5000 people 30 waggons 8 carages 100 struck comensed on fridaye ended on wednesdaye the 2^d saboth of this instant was appointed at blew spring Mr Marshals congration 5000 people 300 comunicants a stout helthe man aged 30 said that if he fell being there at a meeting he wished that some person would put thier feet on him by the way of derishon he was struck down alltho a daye before acknowledge himselfe a grait sinour and that salvation can be had now other way than through christ alltho had not got a hope

this extrodenery woork is not alltogether confined to the presbeterian sosciteye it appears among the Methodists and Babtis the folowing is a few extrodenery cases at the occasion at point plesent a man upwards of fifty in oposition had prapered a staf with a sharp nail in the lower end intending when a opertuity served of a crowd would be around some person struck down he would reach the staff through and make them start up by proding them not a minet after warmely disputing with a person who was in favour of the work he fell as dead lay a bout an hour speachless when recovered [he] confesed what his intentions ware and allso what a dredful sinor he was and alltho subject to intoxication for the most part appears since to leave it off and attend to reliegious exercises. a man at point plesent in oposition to the woork was struck down when he came too so as to speak he confesed that he was a drunkard a lyor a thiefe and whiped his wife appaled to his wife and nabours who ware present for the truth of what he said—

one young woman in going to a place of woorship said that if she fell she wished that it might be into hell she was struck down fell stiff heer hand and arm to the allso became as cold as Death heer fingeers cramped recove[d] heer speach in 2 hours was haled home on a sled continues in a state of despare which has lasted 3 weekes

APPENDIX VIII

[Letter from William McKendree[1]]

October 10, 1802.

THROUGH mercy my Life is yet spared, and notwithstanding the labours I have to perform, and the sickliness of some part of my district, I enjoy almost uninterrupted health, for which I desire to be profoundly thankful.

To give you a particular account of the Work of God in the Western Country, would exceed the bounds of a letter, and swell into a Pamphlet, I can therefore give you but a general view of what God is in mercy doing for his People.

My Spring visit ended at our old friend Philip Gatche's Little Miami, on the third Sunday in June, which was the thirteenth Sabbath in continuity that I attended Meetings from two to four days each. Our Congregations were generally large, (in places where fifty formerly made a respectable Congregation, a thousand is now a tolerable gathering) and blessed be God we were generally favoured with distinguishing marks of the divine presence. I introduced the Lime-stone Quarterly meeting, with Rom. i. 16. the LORD was present indeed; we had a most solemn Meeting time. At the Sacrament on the LORD'S day, (which was administered out of doors of necessity,) the LORD was powerfully present; the place was so awful, that the looks of the bystanders visibly proclaimed, "GOD is here and we are afraid."—Psalm lxxxiv. II. was the subject on Monday: The Sermon that day imperceptibly led my mind back to day of Pentcost, for truly, the burst of joy, when it could be restrained no longer, was as the voice of rushing Wind.

[1] *Extracts of Letters* . . . . *Written by Preachers and Members of the Methodist Episcopal Church to Their Bishops*, pp. 39–42.

A few appeared to be angry and withdrew, but the Work continued till near Sunset. It would be mere conjecture to give the number converted.

People came from far to the Miami Quarterly Meeting. I heard of Women that walked thirty miles to it, so that our Congregation was very large for that new country. On the first day we were favoured with the presence of the LORD in a singular manner, and I think I may safely say it increased throughout the Meeting. On Sunday two young Women of genteel appearance, fell not far from the stand, but were presently taken off by some Men, (their brothers as I was informed) The Spirit of GOD, like a Sword, pierced one of the Men, & about ten steps from the stand, he suddenly fell to the Earth, together with his weeping charge, and cried aloud for mercy! The other was graciously visited in like manner; thus there were four instead of two deeply engaged; this attracted the attention of many, so that there were many convicted through their means, and I am informed they never rested until they found Peace, by which means religion was carried into other parts and the Work of GOD continued to spread.

The last thing respecting this Meeting, which I shall mention, is a case of simplicity which deeply affected my mind. An old Woman sitting just behind me while Brother Smith was speaking, began in a low and mournful manner, and expressed herself to the following purport:

"LORD I have heard about these People, and walked a long way to hear them. Yesterday while the Man was speaking I felt very bad, and thought I should fall down, but LORD I was ashamed that the People should see me cry and fall down, so I did not know that it was the LORD. But I could not walk, I fell down among all the People, and all my shame went away! and now I am happly! bless the LORD he has converted my Soul! Oh how light my Heart is now, Glory! Glory to King Jesus! But oh LORD my husband is wicked, my children are wicked! and they must be Converted, and there is no Religion in the Neighbourhood. No one to tell them how to get converted! LORD send some of these Preachers, that have the Spirit of GOD in their hearts, into our Neighbourhood, to my house, to tell the People the way to Heaven."

This Prayer so affected me, that, at that time, I felt willing to preach the Gospel to the Poor in every disconsolate corner.

Our Fall Quarterly Meetings for certain reasons, have uniformly commenced on Friday, and continued until Monday. The Congregations have been large, and I trust the Meetings truly profitable to many. We have an addition of three thousand two hundred and fifty; thus we find that our labours in the Western Conference have been, in some degree blessed this year.

The travelling and located Preachers are sweetly united, and in the Spirit of the Work. In the judgment of many, Methodism never was in so good a state in the western Country as is at present.

There is still a very encouraging prospect of Religion in some of the Presbyterian Congregations.—Some of the Ministers and Members of this order are sweetly united to us in heart and affection, some are friendly, others keep at a distance: and we move on in our order, glad to meet them at all times, on proper ground of Friendship, but when this is denied us, we commit the Ark to GOD, and still drive on.

About two years ago, there was a great ingathering among the Baptists: but they are a strange People. When there was a Work among them it was of the LORD, when it is with the Methodists and Presbyterians, it is of the devil, in the judgement of some of them. They unchurch all other, consider them as unbaptized heathens, refuse Communion with them, and still if they can get one of these into the Water, upon his present experience, they roundly assert he is as sure of Heaven as the happy angels are, and thus make a Saviour of Water.

There is one thing more which I think deserves a thought. According to the reports, there is a great revival of Religions in this country: and we are very sincere Republicans; but alas! as yet their united strength is utterly too weak to abolish Slavery in Kentuky and Cumberland.

Yours, in much Love.

W. M. KENDREE
[Probably a misprint for
W. McKendree]

BIBLIOGRAPHY

THE WEST AT THE END OF THE EIGHTEENTH CENTURY

HOWE, HENRY, *Historical Collections of the Great West* (Cincinnati, 1851).

HOWARD, GEORGE E., *Preliminaries of the Revolution* (1905), in "American Nation" series.

IMLAY, GEORGE, *A Topographical Description of the Western Territory of North America* (London, 1792).

MCLAUGHLIN, ANDREW C., *The Confederation and the Constitution* (1905), in "American Nation" series.

MCMASTER, JOHN B., *A History of the People of the United States*, Vols. I, II, III (New York, 1885–92).

ROOSEVELT, THEODORE, *The Winning of the West* (4 vols., 1889–96).

United States Census Report for 1800.

VAN TYNE, Claude H., *The American Revolution* (1905), in "American Nation" series.

STATE HISTORIES

KENTUCKY

BRIDEL, LOUIS, *Le Pour et Le Contre, ou Avis à ceux qui se proposent de passer dans les États-Unis d'Amérique, suivi d'une description du Kentucky et du Genesy* (Basle, 1803).

BROWN, JOHN MASON, *The Political Beginnings of Kentucky* (Louisville, 1889).

DRAKE, DANIEL, *Pioneer Life in Kentucky, A Series of Letters* (Cincinnati, 1870).

BUTLER, MANN, *History of Kentucky to 1813* (Cincinnati, 1836).

MARSHALL, HUMPHREY, *History of Kentucky* (2 vols., 1812).

TENNESSEE

CARR, JOHN, *Early Times in Middle Tennessee* (Nashville, 1857).

PHELAN, JAMES, *History of Tennessee* (1889).

PUTNAM, A. W., *History of Middle Tennessee, Or Life and Times of General James Robertson* (Nashville, 1857).

SOUTH CAROLINA

DODDRIDGE, JOSEPH, *Notes on the Settlement and Indian Wars of Western Virginia and Pennsylvania, 1763–1783.* Together with a view of the state of society, and manners of the first settlers of the western country (ed. A. Williams, Albany, 1876).

KERCHIVAL, SAMUEL, *A History of the Valley of Virginia* (Woodstock, Va., 1850).

RAMSAY, DAVID, *The History of South Carolina, 1670–1808* (2 vols., Charleston, 1809).

GEOGRAPHY

BRADLY, ABRAHAM, JR., *Map of the United States*, 1804.

CAREY and LEA, *Atlas*, 1800, 1822; *Pocket Atlas*, 1801.

MORSE, JEDIDIAH, *The American Geography* (London, 1792).

SEMPLE, ELLEN C., *American History and Its Geographic Conditions* (1904).

Statistical Atlas of the United States, 1900.

DENOMINATIONAL HISTORY

GENERAL

The "American Church History" series (13 vols., 1893–97).

DORCHESTER, DANIEL, *Christianity in the United States* (New York, 1890).

RUPP, ISRAEL D., *Original History of the Religious Denominations at Present Existing in the United States* (Philadelphia, 1844).

PRESBYTERIAN

BISHOP, ROBERT H., *Outline History of the Church in the State of Kentucky, 1783-1823. . . . . Memoirs of Rev. David Rice* (Lexington, 1824).

DAVIDSON, ROBERT, *History of the Presbyterian Church in the State of Kentucky* (New York, 1847).

GILLETT, E. H., *History of the Presbyterian Church in the United States* (2 vols., 1864).

KENNEDY, WILLIAM S., *The Plan of Union; Or a History of the Presbyterian and Congregational Churches of the Western Reserve, with Biographical Sketches of the Early Missionaries* (Hudson, Ohio, 1856).

SMITH, JOSEPH, *Old Redstone, Or Historical Sketches of Western Presbyterianism and Its Early Ministers* (Philadelphia, 1854).

Minutes of the General Assembly, 1789-1820 (Philadelphia, 1847).

Mss Minutes of the Presbytery of Transylvania.

CUMBERLAND PRESBYTERIAN

McDONNOLD, B. W., *History of the Cumberland Presbyterian Church* (Nashville, 1893).

SMITH, JAMES, *History of the Christian Church, Including a History of the Cumberland Presbyterian Church* (1835).

BAPTIST

ASPLUND, JOHN, *The Annual Register of the Baptist Denomination in North America to the First of November 1790* (Southampton Co., Va., 1791); *The Universal Register of the Baptist Denomination in North America, 1790-1-2-3-4* (Boston, 1794).

BENEDICT, DAVID, *A General History of the Baptist Denomination in America, and Other Parts of the World* (2 vols., Boston, 1813); *Abridgement and Continuation of the General History* (2 vols. in one, New York, 1850); *Fifty Years among the Baptists* (New York, 1860).

BURKITT, LEMUEL, and READ, JESSE, *A Concise History of the Kehukee Baptist Association from Its Original Rise to the Present Time* (Halifax, 1803).

DUNLEVY, A. H., *History of the Miami Baptist Association from Its Organization in 1797 to a Division . . . . in 1836* (Cincinnati, 1869).

RILEY, B. F., *History of the Southern Baptists East of the Mississippi* (Philadelphia, 1898).

SEMPLE, ROBERT B., *A History of the Rise and Progress of the Baptists in Virginia* (Richmond, 1810; G. B. Beale ed., 1894).

SMITH, JUSTIN A., *History of the Baptists in the Western States East of the Mississippi* (Philadelphia, 1896).

TAYLOR, JAMES B., *Lives of Virginia Baptist Ministers* (Richmond, 1838).

TAYLOR, JOHN, *History of Ten Baptist Churches* (Frankfort, 1823).

METHODIST

ATKINSON, JOHN, *Centennial History of American Methodism* (New York, 1884).

BANGS, NATHAN, *History of the Methodist Episcopal Church* (4 vols., New York, 1857).

BENNETT, WILLIAM W., *Memorials of Methodism in Virginia* (Richmond, 1871).

BUCKLEY, JAMES M., *A History of Methodism in the United States* (2 vols., New York, 1898).

FINLEY, J. B., *Sketches of Western Methodism* (Cincinnati, 1854).

GARRETT, L., *Recollections of the West* (Nashville, 1834).

GORRIE, P. DOUGLASS, *The Lives of Eminent Methodist Ministers* (Auburn, 1852).
LEE, JESSE, *A Short History of the Methodists in the United States of America, 1766–1809* (Baltimore, 1810).
MCFERRIN, J. B., *History of the Methodists in Tennessee* (3 vols., Nashville, 1869).
PRICE, R. N., *Holston Methodism* (3 vols., Nashville, 1904–8).
REDFORD, A. H., *The History of Methodism in Kentucky* (3 vols., Nashville, 1868–70).
STEVENS, ABEL, *History of the Methodist Episcopal Church* (4 vols., New York, 1864–67).

AUTOBIOGRAPHY AND BIOGRAPHY

Rev. Joseph Badger, A Memoir of, Containing an Autobiography and Selections from His Private Journal and Correspondence (Hudson, Ohio, 1851).
H. Boehm, Reminiscences, History, and Biography of Sixty-four Years in the Ministry (ed. Joseph B. Wakeley, New York, 1865).
Rev. William Burke, Autobiography of (Finley, *Sketches of Western Methodism*).
Peter Cartwright the Backwoods Preacher, Autobiography of (ed. William P. Strickland, London, 1858).
Rev. John Clark, "Father Clark," by an Old Pioneer (New York, 1855).
Rev. Thomas Coke, The Life of, Samuel Drew (London, 1817).
Rev. George Donnell, Life of, F. C. Anderson (Nashville, 1858).
Rev. Finis Ewing, Life and Times of, F. R. Cossitt (1853).
Rev. James B. Finley, Autobiography of (ed. William P. Strickland, Cincinnati, 1867).
Rev. Robert Finley, Memoirs of . . . . with Brief Sketches of Some of His Contemporaries, Isaac V. Brown (New Brunswick, 1819).

Rev. William Hickman, Autobiography of (MSS, Durrett Collection, 1838).

Rev. Jesse Lee, Life of, L. M. Lee (Richmond, 1848).

Eld. Barton W. Stone, The Biography of, Written by Himself with Additions and Reflections, by Elder John Rogers (Cincinnati, 1853). Also found in *The Cane Ridge Meeting-House,* James R. Rogers (Cincinnati, 1910).

Rev. Jacob Young, Autobiography of a Pioneer, Or the Nativity, Experience, Travels, and Ministerial Labors of (Cincinnati, 1860).

JOURNALS AND TRAVELS

Rev. Francis Asbury, The Journal of, 1771–1815 (3 vols., New York, 1821).

BAILY, FRANCIS, *Journal of a Tour in Unsettled Parts of North America, 1796, 1797* (London, 1856).

BAYARD, F. M., *Voyages dans l'intérieur des États-Unis à Bath, Winchester, dans la Vallée de Shenandoah . . . . Pendant l'été 1797* (Paris, 1798).

BIRKBECK, MORRIS, *Notes on a Journey in America, Virginia to the Territory of Illinois* (Philadelphia, 1817).

BRADBURY, JOHN, *Travels in the Interior of America, Including a Description of Upper Louisiana, together with the States of Ohio, Kentucky, Indiana and Tennessee with the Illinois and Western Territories, in the Years 1809, 1810 and 1811* (Liverpool, 1817).

CUMING, F., *Sketches of a Tour to the Western Country through the States of Ohio and Kentucky . . . . , 1807–1809* (Pittsburgh, 1810).

Manasseh Cutler, Life, Journals and Correspondence of, by William Cutler and Julia P. Cutler (2 vols., 1888).

DAVIS, JOHN, *Travels of Four and One-Half Years in the United States of America, during 1798, 1799, 1800, 1801, and 1802* (Bristol, 1803).

Andrew Ellicott, Journal of, ... during Part of the Year 1796, the Years 1797, 1798, and Part of the Year 1800 (Philadelphia, 1814).

ESPY, JOSIAH, *A Tour in Ohio, Kentucky and Indiana Territory*, 1805.

FEARON, H. B., *Sketches of America; A Journal through the Eastern and Western States, 1817* (London, 1818).

FLINT, JAMES, *Letters from America* (Edinburgh, 1822).

FLINT, TIMOTHY, *Recollections of the Last Ten Years Passed in Occasional Residences and Journeys in the Valley of the Mississippi* (a series of letters, Boston, 1826).

HARRIS, THADDEUS M., *The Journal of a Tour into the Territory North-west of the Alleghany Mountains; Made in the Spring of the Year 1803* (Boston, 1805).

MELISH, JOHN, *Travels in the United States of America, 1806, 1807, 1809–1811* (2 vols., Philadelphia, 1812).

MICHAUX, F. A., *Travels to the Westward of the Alleghany Mountains in the States of the Ohio, Kentucky, and Tennessee and Return to Charlestown . . . . 1802* (London, 1805).

MILLS, SAMUEL J., and SMITH, DANIEL, *Report of a Missionary Tour through That Part of the United States Which Lies West of the Alleghany Mountains, 1814–1815* (Andover, 1815).

SCHERMERHORN, J. F., and MILLS, S. J., *A Correct View of That Part of the United States Which Lies West of the Alleghany Mountains, with Regard to Religion and Morals* (Hartford, 1814).

SHULTZ, C. J., *Travels in New York, Pennsylvania, Virginia, Ohio, Kentucky, Tennessee, Indiana, ... 1807, 1808* (2 vols., New York, 1810).

WELD, I., *Travels in North America and Canada* (London, 1799).

REVIVAL LITERATURE

Extracts of Letters Containing Some Account of the Work of God since 1800 Written by Preachers and Members of the Methodist Episcopal Church to Their Bishops (Barnard, Vt., 1812).

GALLAHER, JAMES, *The Western Sketch Book* (Boston, 1850).

Rev. John Lyle, Diary of (typewritten copy, Durrett Collection, University of Chicago Library).

Gospel News or a Brief Account of the Revival of Religion in Kentucky and Several Other Parts of the United States. .... (Baltimore, Md., 1801).

HUMPHREY, HEMAN, *Revival Sketches and Manual* (New York, 1859).

James McGready, The Posthumous Works of (2 vols., ed. Rev. James Smith, Louisville, 1831).

LIVINGSTON, JOHN H., *Sermon before the New York Missionary Society, at Their Annual Meeting, April 3, 1804*, Appendix, and *Other Papers Relating to American Missions* (Greenfield, 1809).

McNEMAR, RICHARD, *The Kentucky Revival* (Cincinnati, 1808).

MSS Letters in the Draper Collection (Library of The State Historical Society of Wisconsin).

MARCH, ANGIER, *Increase of Piety or the Revival of Religion in the United States of America Containing Several Interesting Letters Not Before Published* (Newburyport, 1802).

RICE, DAVID, *A Sermon on the Present Revival of Religion .... Preached at the Opening of the Kentucky Synod* (Lexington, Ky., 1804).

SPEER, WILLIAM, *The Great Revival of 1800* (1872).

SPRAGUE, W. B., *Lectures on Revivals of Religion* (1833).

STILLMAN, SAMUEL, *A Discourse Preached in Boston before the Massachusetts Baptist Missionary Society, May 25, 1803. Being Their First Anniversary* (Boston, 1803).

STONE, BARTON W., *An Address to the Christian Churches in Kentucky, Tennessee, and Ohio on Several Important Doctrines of Religion* (Lexington, 1821).

PERIODICALS

The American Pioneer, 1842, 1843 (Cincinnati).
Biblical Repertory, 1834.
Connecticut Evangelical Magazine, 1800–1807 (Hartford).
Magazine of Western History, 1884–94.
Massachusetts Missionary Magazine, 1803–8 (Salem).
Massachusetts Baptist Missionary Magazine, 1803–10 (Boston).
New York Missionary Magazine, 1800–1803 (New York). Especially valuable, contains "McGready's Narrative of the Great Revival in Logan County and many interesting letters describing the revivals at this time in various parts of the United States.
Weekly Recorder, 1814–16 (Chillicothe, Ohio).

THE REVIVAL AND SLAVERY

BIRNEY, WILLIAM, *James G. Birney and His Times. The Genesis of the Republican Party with Some Accounts of the Abolition Movements in the South before 1828* (New York, 1890).

LOCKE, MARY S., *Anti-Slavery in America from the Introduction of African Slaves to the Prohibition of the Slave Trade, 1619–1808* (Boston, 1901).

PSYCHOLOGY OF THE REVIVAL

AMES, EDWARD S., *The Psychology of Religious Experience* (Boston, 1910).

CARPENTER, WILLIAM B., *Principles of Mental Physiology* (New York 1894).

DAVENPORT, FREDERICK M., *Primitive Traits in Religious Revivals* (New York, 1905).

JAMES, WILLIAM, *The Principles of Psychology* (2 vols.); *The Varieties of Religious Experience* (New York, 1902).

LE BON, GUSTAVE, *The Crowd, A Study of the Popular Mind* (London, 1900).

MAUDSLEY, HENRY, *Physiology of Mind* (1889).

ROBINS, ELIZABETH, "Maenadism in Religion," *Atlantic Monthly*, Vol. LII, 487–97.

STOLL, OTTO, *Suggestion und Hypnotismus in der Völkerpsychologie* (Leipzig, 1894).

WHITE, ANDREW D., "Diabolism and Hysteria," *Popular Science Monthly*, Vol. XXXV, 1–16, 145–55.

www.ingramcontent.com/pod-product-compliance
Lightning Source LLC
Chambersburg PA
CBHW070735160426
43192CB00009B/1448